Contents

Contributors

Philip Yancey is editor-at-large for *Christianity Today*. He is co-author, with Paul Brand, of *Fearfully and Wonderfully Made* and *In His Image*, and author of a number of other books.

Becky Pippert is the author of *Out of the Saltshaker: Evangelism as a Way of Life*, and *Hope has its Reasons.*

J. I. Packer is the author of *Knowing God*, and many other books. He is currently Sangwoo Youtong Chee Professor of Theology at Regent College, in Vancouver, Canada.

Elisabeth Elliot is the author of *Through Gates of Splendour*, and many other books. Her first husband, Jim Elliot, along with four other missionaries, was speared to death by Auca Indians in Ecuador.

Charles Colson, who served as Special Counsel to President Richard M. Nixon from 1969 to 1973, is president and founder of Prison Fellowship. His associate Ellen Santilli Vaughn collaborated on his chapter in this book.

Preface

Each person enters life with an inheritance, a legacy, if you will. Listen to the family's remarks when a baby comes home from the hospital. His dimpled chin looks just like Uncle Harold's. Her delicate fingers are exactly like her sister Ellen's.

In truth, each of us arrives in this world with certain characteristics inherited from our parents and their parents before them. This inheritance profoundly shapes our life and identity. And in these things we have no choice.

But there is another inheritance that does come to us by choice. It is the Christian inheritance that becomes ours when we give our lives to Christ and are called by his name. Even so, it is an inheritance which comes to us now only in part. It is a promise not fully realized until the life to come. Meanwhile, as Paul says in Philippians, we 'press on towards the goal for the prize of the upward call of God in Christ Jesus'.

Part of this striving, this pressing on towards the goal, involves the struggle to become better persons, to penetrate the darkness that threatens to envelop the world around us. It will help us in this struggle to look for real people, fellow Christians who, though flawed in heart and mind, have nonetheless given their all to God and emerged as individuals who can light the way ahead. It is simply good sense to learn from other Christians about the perils that face us and the rewards that await us. It can be tremendously encouraging to realize from their examples that we can succeed – and succeed gloriously – despite the obstacles.

With this in mind we posed the following question to each of the contributors to this book: 'Would you write about someone you particularly admire, a person remarkable for his or her Christian heroism?' The response was enthusiastic – and varied. The contributors have written chapters about a doctor, a businesswoman, a preacher, a missionary and a social reformer. As varied as the circumstances of these men and women were, their lives of courage, love, and faithfulness speak powerfully of the one they followed.

This is not to imply that they were perfect people. On the contrary, each of these men and women had to contend against external and internal obstacles – their own pride, stubbornness, discouragement, and doubts. But through it all God has made them better persons, stronger Christians, heroes to be followed.

Dwight Moody said, 'Character is what you are in the dark.' Certainly many of these people faced the darkest circumstances, and the contributors have not tried to hide the dark or to magnify the light in the lives of those they write about. Their goal was only to tell the truth. As a result, we learn not only about the men and women whose stories they tell but also about the authors themselves – their hopes, struggles, and deepest ideals.

This, then, is the inheritance we share and, through the grace of God, pass on to others.

Ann Spangler
Charles Turner

Paul Brand

by Philip Yancey

I first met Dr Paul Brand in the grounds of the official US Public Health Service leprosarium in Carville, Louisiana. To get there, I drove from New Orleans for two hours along the levéed banks of the Mississippi River, past crumbling old plantations, crawfish cafés and gleaming new petrochemical factories. The Catholic sisters who had drained the swamps and built the hospital buildings a hundred years before had deliberately located them away from major population centres. Laid out in a sprawling, colonial style under huge oak trees, Carville resembled the film set of a Philippine plantation.

I knew of Dr Brand's stature in the world medical community: the offers to head up major medical centres, the distinguished lectureships in Great Britain and America, the surgical procedures named after him, the prestigious Albert Lasker award, his designation as Commander of the Order of the British Empire. But I waited for him in a cubbyhole of an office hardly suggestive of such renown. Stacks of medical journals, photographic slides, and unanswered correspondence covered every square inch of an ugly government-green metal desk. An antique window air-conditioner throbbed at the decibel level of an unmuffled sports car. Charts of the labyrinthine government bureaucracy, not awards and citations, covered his office walls.

Finally, a slight man of less than average height entered the room. He had grey hair, bushy eyebrows, and a face that creased deeply when he smiled. In an English accent, a striking contrast to the bayou accents heard in the hospital corridors, he apologized for the flecks of blood on his lab coat, explaining that he had just been dissecting rabbit muscles.

That first visit to Dr Brand lasted a week. We grabbed bits of conversations between management meetings, surgeries, clinical lectures, and animal research. I accompanied him on hospital rounds, leaving a wide berth in the hallways for the whirring electric wheelchairs and bicycles jerry-rigged with sidecars and extra wheels. I sat in the examination room as he studied the inflamed, ulcerated feet and hands of patients, trying to coax from them the cause of their injuries.

At night in his home, a rented wooden-frame bungalow in the grounds of the hospital, I would share an Indian-style meal with him and Mrs Brand (also a doctor). Then Dr Brand would prop up his bare feet (a trademark with him), and I would turn on the tape recorder for discussions that ranged from leprology and theology to world hunger and soil conservation.

In my role as editor of *Campus Life* magazine and writer for other magazines, I had interviewed many subjects over the years: rock music stars, successful business people, Pulitzer Prize winners and Olympic athletes. Something, however, attracted me to Dr Brand at a deeper level than I had felt with any other interview subject. I found in him a rich mixture of compassion, scientific precision, theological depth, and spiritual humility. In addition, his ideas on pain and pleasure were utterly different from any I had encountered in months of research.

My visit to Carville sparked a relationship that has grown and developed ever since. Later, when I left *Campus Life* to pursue freelance writing, I devoted the first five years to presenting the fruits of our dialogue: first in *Where is God when it Hurts?*, and then in two books we co-authored, *Fearfully and Wonderfully Made* and *In His Image*. I still maintain file folders labelled 'Brand' stuffed with unused notes on topics we have never explored in print.

True friendship is measured, over time, by its effect on you. Has the association in some way changed your essential nature? As I compare the person I was in 1975, on our first meeting, and the person I am now, I realize that seismic changes have occurred within me, and Dr Brand has been responsible for many of those tremors.

I was a college student during the 1960s. That tumultuous era awakened me to the ugly reality of poverty in the third world and in American ghettos. Everything in America seemed to be cracking apart in those days: the Vietnam war chiselled away at our national ideals (and later Watergate proved the political cynics correct), revelations about pollution and the environment challenged the industrial ethic that had built our country, and the new counter-culture exposed the hollow, image-conscious materialism that permeated business and the media. The issues are now so familiar as to become hackneyed. But to those of us who were forming a view of the world in that era, the sixties had a profound and permanent impact.

I recall my emotions in those years as being primarily anger, loneliness, and despair. I felt drawn towards books about the Holocaust, the Soviet Gulag, and other black holes of human history. I saw bright and talented friends give up on society and seek a different way through LSD and mescaline. Examining the church from such a jaded perspective, I noted mainly the hypocrisy of its members and their irrelevance to the world outside.

I now believe that God used Dr Brand as one of his human agents to bring me out of that time with some stability. I was twenty-five when we first met; he was sixty. We made an odd pair, he with thinning grey hair and I with bushy hair in an Afro style. But somehow our friendship flourished. I look with deep appreciation on the privilege of learning from a great and humble man. I came to know him not through history, but as an actual living model, a man of God I could see in action – at Carville with his patients, in rural villages in India, as a husband and father, as a speaker at both medical and spiritual conferences. He, as much as anyone, has helped set my course in attitude, spirit, and ideals. In this tribute, I hope to identify partially how he has done so.

Dr Brand achieved fame in the medical world mainly through his pioneering research on the disease leprosy. He had grown up in southern India, a child of missionary parents, and returned in 1946 after being educated in England. During eighteen years in India he worked as a surgeon and teacher, directed the large Christian Medical College Hospital in Vellore, and founded a leprosy hospital known as Karigiri. Then, in 1965, he moved to the United States and began research work at the Carville hospital.

I did not expect to find gratitude as the chief characteristic of a man who had spent his life among victims of leprosy. Through the medical ignorance of others, those afflicted by leprosy are often isolated and reviled. In a place such as India, they are the outcasts of society, often doubly so as members of the untouchable caste.

Leprosy disproportionately afflicts the poor. Left untreated, its victims can develop the nerve damage and ulcers that eventually lead to facial disfigurement and loss of limbs. If anyone has a right to bitterness against the way the world is run, it should be someone who works with these unfortunates. And yet the single characteristic that most impressed me about Dr Brand was his bedrock of gratitude.

For Paul Brand, gratitude began in childhood as simple appreciation of the natural world around him. He grew up in remote hill country, with none of civilization's normal barriers against nature. Snakes lived in the dark corners of the house and leopards stalked the forests outside, but apart from these dangers nature seemed wholly good. Until the age of nine he did his schoolwork sitting on a branch of a giant tamarind tree, dropping his completed assignments down to his mother on the ground below.

He spent childhood in a world of tropical fruit trees and of butterflies, insects, birds, and other animals. His artistic mother tried to capture its beauty visually, sometimes calling wildly to him to come and look at the sunset as she daubed paints on a canvas.

His father, a self-taught naturalist, saw nature as an awesome display of the genius of the creator. He would lead his son to a towering four-feet-high termite mound and carefully expose the elaborate network of passages and their built-in cooling system, explaining the marvels of co-operative termite society. He would point to the sandy funnel of an ant lion trap, or the nest of a weaver bird, or a swarm of bees hanging from a tree.

The need for education interrupted Paul Brand's paradise, and he was sent to England at the age of nine. Five years later, as a fourteen-year-old student far from his native homeland, he received a telegram that his father had died of blackwater fever. Two days after the telegram, a letter from his father arrived, sent by boat before his death. It described the hills around their home:

> Yesterday when I was riding over the windswept hilltops around Kulivalavu, I could not help thinking of an old hymn that begins, 'Heaven above is deeper blue; flowers with purer beauty glow.' When I am alone on these long rides, I love the sweet smelling wood, the dear brown earth, the lichen on the rocks, the heaps of dead brown leaves drifted like snow in the hollows. God means us to delight in his world. It isn't necessary to know botany or zoology or biology in order to enjoy the manifold life of nature. Just observe. And remember. And compare. And be always looking to God with thankfulness and worship for having placed you in such a delightful corner of the universe as the planet Earth.

Jesse Brand's son kept his advice, and keeps it to this day, whether hiking on the Olympic Peninsula or following birds around the swamps of Louisiana.

Another naturalist, the author Loren Eiseley, tells of an event he called the most significant learning experience of his long life. Caught on a beach in a sudden rainstorm, he sought shelter under a huge piece of driftwood. There, he found a tiny fox cub, maybe ten weeks old. The cub had no fear of humans. Within a few minutes it had engaged Eiseley in a playful game of tug of war, with Eiseley holding one end of a chicken bone in his mouth and the baby fox pulling on the other end.

The lesson he learned, said Eiseley, is that at the core of the universe, the face of God is a smile. Even the most ferocious animals – leopards and grizzly bears and rhinoceroses – begin their lives playfully. Paul Brand, too, learned that lesson early. First in the hills of India, and later through a detailed study of the human body, he came to realize that at the heart of the natural world God could be found, and the God that he found was good.

Brand gained a sense of creatureliness, an awareness that he too had been willed into existence by a loving creator and placed on a planet that, despite all its pain and fear, contained much beauty and goodness. He began to develop a consistent outlook of gratitude, undergirded by trust in the one who made the world.

My early conversations with Brand, coming as they did out of a time of personal searching, focused mainly on the dark spots and blemishes on the world. How could a truly good God allow such blemishes to exist? Dr Brand took them on one by one. Disease? Did I know that 99 per cent of all bacteria are beneficial, not harmful? Plants could not produce oxygen and animals could not digest food without the assistance of bacteria. Most agents of disease, he explained, diverge from these necessary organisms by only slight mutations.

What about birth defects? He went on to describe in detail the complex chemical changes that must work correctly to produce one healthy child. The great wonder is not that birth defects exist but that millions more do not occur. Could a mistake-proof world have been created so that DNA spirals would never err in transmission? No scientist could envisage such a system without possibility of error in our world of physical laws.

Even at its worst, he continued, our natural world shows evidence of careful design. Imagine a world without tornadoes or hurricanes, calamities that carry the damning label 'acts of God'. When hurricanes and monsoons do not come, the delicate balance of weather conditions gets upset, and killer droughts inevitably follow. 'How would you improve upon the world? he asked.

Brand's professional life has centred on perhaps the most problematic aspect of creation, the existence of pain. He emphatically insists on pain's great value, holding up as proof the terrible results of leprosy – damaged face, blindness, and loss of fingers, toes and limbs – which nearly all occur as side-effects of the inability to feel pain. Leprosy destroys nerve endings that carry pain signals. People who do not feel pain almost inevitably damage themselves; infection sets in, and no pain signals alert them to tend to the wounded area.

'Thank God for pain!' Brand declares with the utmost sincerity. 'I cannot think of a greater gift I could give my leprosy patients.' (Actually, he tried to give them the protective gift, in a three-year research programme to manufacture an artificial pain system.) Even in this instance, so commonly held up as a challenge to a loving God, he sees reason for profound gratitude.

The Bible records a dramatic scene when the overwhelming questions raised by the problem of pain were asked of God himself, in the Book of Job. The long speech God gave in reply has endured as one of the great nature passages in literature, a wonderful celebration of wildness as seen in mountain goats, ostriches, wild horses and snowstorms. But to the problem of pain God gave no direct answer, only this challenge to Job: if I, as creator, have produced such a marvellous world as this, which you can plainly observe, cannot you trust me with those areas you cannot comprehend?

In that spirit, Dr Brand learned at an early age that God wanted from him gratitude and trust – gratitude for those things he could see and appreciate, and trust regarding those things he could not. To his surprise, that attitude in him deepened even as he worked among people least likely to feel gratitude: the poorest of the poor, leprosy victims in India. In many of them, he saw the transformations that the love of God can produce. The immense human problems he lived among did not dissolve, but his faith supplied a confidence and trust that enabled him to serve God with gratitude and even joy.

Although I have great respect for Dr Brand and his service to God, I also confess relief that he is not from the mould of St Francis or Mother Teresa. I have immense respect for those rare individuals in history who have lived on a different plane, forsaking all material possessions, withdrawing from the world, and devoting themselves single-mindedly to a prophetic ideal. I learn much from them. And yet as I study their lives I sometimes have the nagging sense that they do not live in my world.

In his lifestyle, Dr Brand has chosen the middle way of balancing the material and the mystical, the prophetic and the pragmatic. At the hospital he left behind in Vellore, Brand is remembered for his spiritual depth and sacrificial service, but also for his practical jokes, love for marmalade and mangoes, and fast driving. As I emerged from the sixties, a decade never accused of possessing a sense of balance, I needed an example of someone who lived a well-rounded life in the midst of modern society, not in a monastery or *ashram.* Dr Brand had struggled with both extremes of the tensions facing modern civilization, while not giving in to either. On the one hand, he lived an 'alternative' lifestyle long before such a word entered our vocabulary. The Brand family eats simply, relying mainly on home-made bread and vegetables grown in their garden. Dr Brand acknowledges a few reasons for discarding clothes – unpatchable tears, for instance – but lack of stylishness is certainly not one of them. Furniture in his home and office is, to put it kindly, unpretentious.

On the other hand, he has learned to use the tools made available by modern technology. Under his leadership, a hospital in the dusty backwater town of Vellore grew into the most modern and sophisticated facility in all of south-west Asia. Later, Brand came to the Carville hospital in the United States because it offered the technological support needed to research treatment procedures that would benefit millions of leprosy patients world-wide. And when personal computers were introduced in the 1980s, he signed up with boyish enthusiasm for one of the first IBMs, to assist his research and writing.

My conversations with Dr Brand have often strayed to the question of lifestyle, for his experiences in India and America have afforded him a unique perspective on that issue. He has lived in one of the poorest countries and one of the richest. Affluence in the West, he recognizes, offers a deadly temptation. The enormous gap in economic development can create a moat separating the West from the rest of the world. Wealth can dull us to cries of need and justice, and too much comfort can sap the life from Christian work.

The lifelong tension over lifestyle goes back to Brand's childhood in India. After her husband's death, Paul's mother, Evelyn (Granny) Brand, took on the life of a 'saint' in the traditional form. She lived on a pittance, devoting her life to reach villagers in five mountain ranges. She cared nothing for her personal appearance, not even allowing a mirror in her house. She continued making hazardous journeys on her pony even after suffering concussions and fractures from falls. Although tropical diseases ravaged her body, she gave all her energies to treating the diseases and injuries of the people around her.

Sometimes Granny Brand would embarrass Paul with an intemperate outburst. At an official function in Vellore, for example, she might ask in horror, 'How could you possibly dine on such fine food when I have people back in the hills starving to death this very night!' She died at the age of ninety-five among the people she loved, leaving Paul an unforgettable legacy. (The book *Granny Brand* tells her full story.)

From childhood Paul learned that Christian love is best applied person-to-person. His parents travelled from village to village, teaching health, sanitation, farming, and the Christian gospel. They left behind no lasting institutions, only their permanent imprint on thousands of lives. Single-handedly, Granny Brand rid huge areas of a guinea worm infection that had persisted for centuries. Trusting villagers followed her instructions on building stone walls around their wells; no government programme could have been so effective.

Yet Paul Brand himself found his most lasting successes through rigid scientific disciplines. At Vellore he fought his wife Margaret for space in the fridge, preserving cadaver hands to study by lamplight and practise surgical techniques. For years he puzzled over the physiology of leprosy: which cells does it attack, and why?

His most important medical discovery came when he observed that the leprosy bacillus did not destroy hands and feet but only attacked nerve tissue. Proving that theory required years of painstaking research. He had to keep track of patients and their injuries, searching whether all damage could indeed be traced to abuse of tissue, rather than the disease itself. The results of such research had a dramatic impact on the treatment of leprosy and other anaesthetic diseases worldwide. Fifteen million victims of leprosy gained hope that, with proper care, they could preserve their toes and fingers and limbs. Damage was no longer inevitable.

Brand admits he would shed no tears if all advances from the industrial revolution onward suddenly disappeared – he prefers the simple village life in India, close to the outdoors. Yet unlike, say, Gandhi, he does not want to roll back modern civilization. He gratefully uses electron microscopes and thermograms and aeroplanes.

I sense in him a sort of 'holy indifference' to many of the specifics that bother some sensitive Christians. He opposes waste in all forms. If an item is advertised as 'disposable', he either refuses to buy it or else enjoys finding ways to make it last and last. He lives a remarkably disciplined and simple life. Yet, he says, 'like the apostle Paul, I have learned to be abased and to abound'. To him technology, when used wisely and not destructively, offers a tool that helps advance the goals of the Kingdom.

A similar kind of balance characterizes other areas of Brand's life. His Christian faith developed through a combination of his parents' devout belief and his scientific training in medical school. The church he attended in England, a member of the 'Strict and Particular Baptist' denomination, had not adequately equipped him for intellectual challenges to his faith. But his missionary parents had demonstrated love in action, and although he found no quick answers, his faith remained intact as he deferred the questions to a later date, when he could approach them with more wisdom.

Originally, Brand had planned to go to India as a missionary builder, until an unlikely series of circumstances caused by the Second World War landed him in medical school. He traces much of his spiritual formation to the period of time just before medical school when he signed on for a year with an austere organization called the Missionary Training Colony. The Colony sought to equip missionaries for any rigorous situation they might encounter. It assigned students to live in crude huts, each of which accommodated twelve trainees. Brand's hut had hand-hewn furniture and a tiny charcoal stove which hardly sufficed in the British winter.

The Colony used a simple method of Bible training: each group of twelve trainees would work through the

Bible in two years, wrestling with the issues they found there. No classes in theology and homiletics were held – Colony directors believed the Bible alone supplied all that was needed for theology and living. At regular intervals, the trainees would go out into cities and towns to conduct services, open-air meetings, and camp programmes. Pre-war Britain offered unusual opportunities for confrontational evangelism; sometimes Brand would find his open-air service sandwiched in between a communist rally and a meeting of black-shirt fascists.

Each summer the Colony also sent the groups of twelve 'on trek' for a period of ten weeks without a break; a programme designed to teach teamwork and endurance. Brand's team loaded a two-wheel cart with clothes, tents, and all their necessary belongings. The boys harnessed themselves to the cart with long tow-ropes and marched along the backroads of Britain, singing as they went. When they reached a town in the afternoon, they would check with local church authorities for permission to conduct meetings in the church or in the town square. They slept in tents or on the floors of churches. In ten weeks, Brand's team covered 600 miles up and down the border of England and Wales.

Looking back, Dr Brand fondly recalls that ten-week course as one of the great experiences of his life. It gave him a living, working example of the Body of Christ in action, with each member dependent on the others. Also, it taught him about his own cynicism, and about faith.

The Colony had one absolute rule for the trek: it must be conducted on faith. Each team began the trek with just enough cash to feed them for two or three days if no money or food came in. Otherwise, they depended entirely on what people gave to them, and they were never allowed to ask for gifts or take a collection. The trek offered a chance for a sincere experiment in faith – for most of the boys at least.

Brand and two others viewed the faith rules of the Colony with considerable scepticism. The forced dependence seemed artificial to them – after all, they had relatives at home who could bail them out if necessary, so why starve for a principle? The three formed a secret club, each hiding away a bit of money. They made plans to sneak away from the group now and then to buy ice cream or a piece of cake.

After two or three such clandestine purchases, Brand and his friends realized they were wrong. The rest of the group was maturing into a deep sense of unity and faith, and the three knew their actions could poison that unity. They stopped their secret activities.

The next weeks offered Brand an unforgettable lesson in faith. After the stores and money supplies had run out, the twelve never knew whether they would have another meal. Yet supplies showed up again and again, offered to them by villagers in astonishingly varied ways. They only missed one meal, a breakfast, but half an hour later a lorry driver stopped beside them by the road and asked if they wanted some fresh melons. He had never done such a thing before.

Brand served as treasurer during the last week of the trek and after final expenses were paid, only three shillings and sixpence remained. As he went to the railway station for final arrangements, one trunk suddenly turned up that had not been paid for. The price? Brand's jaw dropped open as the station-master quoted it: exactly three shillings and sixpence. The group of twelve headed back to the Colony, having never missed a meal, with no money but with a permanent lesson in faith.

The Colony taught Brand a lifelong pattern. He would use his own resources and intelligence as fully as possible but freely acknowledge dependence on God for the ultimate result. Later, in India, he had many opportunities to put faith into practice. The massive building plans at the Vellore hospital were all carried out with no sophisticated appeals for funds. Instead, the staff relied on simple prayer and faith. Brand also learned to seek wisdom from God during important research assignments, or in the midst of surgery. For him, faith became a daily habit that affected every part of his life. He no longer felt a dichotomy between the natural and spiritual realms.

During his time at the Missionary Training Colony, Paul Brand also gained a new perspective on the concept of 'self-sacrifice'. The Colony intentionally created difficult circumstances for its students in order to prepare them for conditions they might encounter on their mission postings.

Primitive living conditions were not new to Brand. As a child, he had lived in a hand-built cabin with no water or electricity in a disease-infested region known as the 'Mountains of Death'. He had regularly fought off bouts of malaria. In bed at night he could hear rats crawling overhead. Yet when he arrived in England for schooling, he quickly saw that his own childhood had been far more adventurous and thrilling than the middle-class environment around him.

Gradually he learned an important part of his life philosophy: that pleasure and pain are not opposites, but rather mutually dependent parts of the richest experiences in life. Most often, the greatest pleasures come after great sacrifice, including considerable pain. The pattern holds true for musicians, who endure tedious hours of practice in order to produce great music, and for athletes, who willingly take on habitual pain in order to condition their bodies. Pleasure derived from producing great music and achieving athletic excellence can come in no other way except through pain.

Brand studied the life of the apostle Paul, who viewed the sufferings he endured in his attempts to preach the gospel as merely the cost required to fulfil his goals. Brand decided to stop looking at life as a polarity: avoid painful experiences, seek pleasurable ones. Rather, he would first ask, 'Is this what God wants me to do?' If so, whatever came along, whether unpleasant or pleasant, provided an opportunity for him to exercise faith. He tried to think of normally unpleasant experiences as something of an adventure.

Brand's family went through trials that would horrify a modern mission executive. His first child was born while he was on wartime duty at a London hospital, fire-watching from the roof in order to dispatch emergency crews to deal with bombing victims. His second came while he was packing for India. He had to leave his wife and children behind in England for six months while he established himself at Vellore (volatile political conditions in India delayed his wife from coming).

Missionary service in India took its own toll. As his body adjusted to a new climate, he broke out in prickly heat in the 110 degree temperatures and suffered through a series of tropical diseases. He practised surgery under a homemade operating lamp hammered out of a sheet of aluminium.

In India, Dr Brand insisted that each of his children (eventually six in all) be brought up with the same freedom and sense of adventure he had known in childhood. Only half in jest, he calculated that it would be far better to have only four of his children live to adulthood than to have all six survive by living sheltered, over-protected lives. He encouraged them to climb, explore, and enjoy fully the adventures that India offered. As the children reached a certain age, the Brands had the wrenching experience of separation, as they sent each child off to England to school. Somehow, the family came through beautifully, and all six children survived.

The pattern I observed in Dr Brand and his family reinforces a trend I have noted among various Christians I have interviewed for magazines. Not everyone fits the pattern, certainly, but I have encountered it so often that I can almost lump these interview subjects into two sets: Christian entertainers and Christian servants. The Christian entertainers – musicians, actors, speakers, comedians – fill our magazines and television shows. We fawn over them, reward them with extravagant contracts and fan mail. They have everything they want, usually, including luxurious lifestyles. Yet many whom I've interviewed express to me deep longings and self-doubts.

In contrast, most of the Christian servants I have interviewed are not in the spotlight. People like the Brands toil unnoticed in remote parts of the country and the world. Relief workers, faithful pastors in communist lands, missionaries in the third world – these have all impressed me with a profound wisdom and deep-seated contentment strikingly absent from the entertainers. They work long hours, for low pay, and no applause. They 'waste' their talents and skills among the poor and uneducated. Yet in the very process of losing their lives, they find them. God reserves rewards for them which are unattainable in any other way.

Dr Brand taught me that self-denial need not be viewed as an affliction, an opportunity for martyrdom. He adamantly refuses to look back on such experiences as sacrifice; they were, rather, challenges, tests of faith. They allowed an opportunity for God to redeem a hopeless situation.

At the hospital in Vellore he encountered seemingly

insurmountable problems. Power failures and equipment breakdowns spoiled many of the research projects. He had to train unskilled Indian workers on the job. Attempts to treat leprosy patients ran into brick walls of opposition – initially, no-one wanted them admitted to the main hospital.

Brand's theories on treatment and rehabilitation had to overcome centuries-old biases about the disease before they gained a foothold in the world medical community. Eventually, he had to find ways to provide new skills, housing, and employment for those leprosy victims who, even upon successful treatment and release, met hostility and rejection in their home villages. Yet, through it all, God's work was accomplished. Today, the leprosy facility at Karigiri flourishes as a world-recognized training centre and its influence has spread to leprosy treatment centres across the globe.

A Christian ministry will require sacrifice – there are no exemptions. Human needs, whether social, spiritual, or physical, will guarantee that. But to a person committed to God, the very aspect of sacrifice can, paradoxically, become one of the most satisfying parts of service.

Dr Brand expresses the guiding principle of his medical career this way: 'The most precious possession any human being has is his spirit, his will to live, his sense of dignity, his personality. Once that has been lost, the opportunity for rehabilitation is lost. Though our profession may be a technical one, concerned with tendons, bones, and nerve endings, we must realize that it is the person behind them who is so important.'

Although our conversations together cover a broad range of topics, inevitably they drift back to stories of individual human beings. The essentials of both his medical philosophy and theology have been worked out through constant contact with patients. Most often, these patients are the forgotten people, the poor and lonely who have been ostracized from family and village because of their illness. A medical team can repair marred facial features and fingers drawn into a claw-hand. They can provide that most basic human need: touch. But what can they do for the spirit of the patient, the corroded self-image?

It takes a few pence a day to arrest leprosy's progress with sulfone drugs. But it takes thousands of pounds and the painstaking care of skilled professionals to restore to wholeness a patient in whom the disease has spread unchecked. In India, Dr Brand began with hands, experimenting with tendon and muscle transfers until he found the very best combination to restore a full range of movement. The surgical procedures and rehabilitation stretched over months and sometimes years. He applied similar procedures to feet, correcting the deformities caused by years of walking without a sense of pain to guide the body in distributing weight and pressure.

New feet and hands gave a leprosy patient the capability to earn a living, but who would hire an employee bearing the scars of the dreaded disease? Brand's first patients returned to him in tears, asking that the effects of surgery be reversed so that they could get more sympathy as beggars. Then Dr Brand and his wife saw the need to correct the cosmetic damage as well. They studied well-known techniques of surgery and modified them for the special problems of leprosy.

They learned to remake a human nose by entering it through the space between the gum and upper lip (to utilize the moist lining inside) and fashioning a new nasal structure from transplanted bone. They learned to prevent blindness by restoring the possibility of blinking: the paralysed eyelid was attached to a muscle normally used for chewing. Margaret Brand worked daily with those patients, teaching them to make a chewing motion with their jaw every thirty seconds, in order to operate their eyelids and thus prevent dehydration of the eye.

Finally, they learned to replace lost eyebrows on the faces of their patients by tunnelling a piece of scalp, intact with its nerve and blood supply, under the skin of the forehead and sewing it in place above the eyes. The first patients proudly let their new eyebrows grow to absurd lengths.

All this elaborate medical care went to 'nobodies', victims of leprosy who most commonly made their living from begging. Many who arrived at the hospital barely looked human. Their shoulders slumped, they cringed when other people approached. Light had faded from their eyes. But months of compassionate treatment from the staff at Vellore could restore that light. For years people had shrunk away from them in terror; at Vellore, nurses and doctors would hold their hands and talk to them. They became human again.

In his twenty years in India, Dr Brand operated on perhaps 3,000 hands and did thousands of other surgical procedures. He cannot possibly recall the details of each patient he come into contact with. Some stand out, however, such as John Kermagan, an irredeemable social misfit who learned of Jesus Christ through Granny Brand. It was the love shown by members of a local church that brought John back to health. He doubted whether any non-patients would accept him, but they did, and thus helped transform his life.

Another patient named John showed up, a near-blind old man with severe damage from the disease. When he begged for surgery to free his stiff hands, Dr Brand hesitated – many younger patients with a full life ahead of them were already waiting for treatment. But the old man got his surgery. Although blind, he somehow learned to play the organ with his insensitive fingers. He spent his last years as official organist at a mission leprosy sanatorium.

There were failures, of course, such as one man who threw himself in a well when he learned two fingers must be amputated. But over time the Brands learned that the human spirit, no matter how battered, can be reawakened and set free. Even in the most ugly, suspicious, hate-filled patients, the image of God began to shine through.

This lesson on the image of God is perhaps the greatest gift Dr Brand has given me. The great societies of the West have been gradually moving away from an underlying belief in the value of a single human soul. We tend to view history in terms of groups of people: classes, political parties, races, sociological groupings. We apply labels to each other, and explain behaviour and ascribe worth on the basis of those labels. After prolonged exposure to Dr Brand, I realized that I had been seeing large human problems as a set of statistics: percentages of Gross National Product, average annual income, mortality rate, doctors-per-thousand of population. I had been wrestling with 'issues' facing 'humanity'. I had not, however, learned to love individuals – people created in the image of God.

I would not have thought of a leprosarium in India as the most likely place to learn about the infinite worth of human beings, but a visit there makes the lesson unavoidable. The love of God is not a matter of statistics; we cannot precisely calculate the greatest possible good to be applied equally to the world's 'poor and needy'. We can only seek out a person, and then another, and then another, as objects for Christian love.

Gratitude, balance, sacrifice, the image of God. In no way have I mastered these principles that Dr Brand has demonstrated for me. I must remind myself of them every day. When I look through my window in the centre of Chicago I ask myself again, How can I be grateful in view of such human misery everywhere? How can I achieve a sense of balance in a world tilting towards chaos? Why should I worry about sacrifice or self-denial when my culture offers me an easier, more pleasurable way? And how can one individual matter? I ask these questions, and perhaps I always will.

But as I ask them, I also give thanks that I have had Dr Brand to help lead me on the way to answers. He would not want me to imply that these qualities have arisen from his own person. The same Holy Spirit that motivated his mother and father in India, and now animates him, is the one who wants to bring adventure and love of life to all who are willing to lose themselves in him. I hope that our collaboration in writing has made it possible for other people to see those same principles and that same Spirit at work in Paul Brand.

Ethel Renwick

by Becky Pippert

If only my parents could find happiness, I thought, then I would be happy too. I was a teenager, watching their marriage dissolve. What I had believed to be the most secure aspect of our life together was in fact the least. But the pain I experienced drove me to ultimate questions. When everything seemed at peace again (although they later divorced), I was still left feeling a strange, gnawing emptiness. I was surprised to realize that what I had longed for the most, a secure family structure, was simply not big enough to build my life upon. So the search began for a foundation strong and trustworthy enough on which to base my life. Although the roots of my search were emotional, the process itself was intellectual.

I studied every system of thought I came across – philosophies, world religions – everything, that is, *except* Christianity. I assumed I knew about Christianity. After all, hadn't I been brought up in America? I had even been a Girl Scout!

Although I was brought up with a great deal of love, ours was not a particularly religious home. I went to

Sunday school and to church sporadically as a young teenager. But evangelical theology and lifestyle were foreign to me.

Everything I studied left me unsatisfied, even despairing. I had wanted logical, defensible answers. I recall asking a believer how he knew his faith was true. 'It's a feeling in my heart,' he said.

'But what about my head? I have a head as well as a heart!' I exclaimed.

Then I stumbled across a book I was surprised to find in my family's library, *Mere Christianity* by C. S. Lewis. In Lewis I found myself face to face with an intellect so disciplined, so lucid, so relentlessly logical, that all of my intellectual pride at not being a 'mindless simple believer' was quickly squelched.

I read Lewis, line by line, with intensity and hunger. The issue finally became clear: Could Jesus really be God? Not a prophet, a great teacher, but *God himself*? My conclusion was twofold: First, if Jesus was God, then the final proof of his God-nature must be his physical resurrection. Secondly, a Christian was one who not only believed in this Jesus, but actually *knew* him. And if those two propositions were true, then as far as I could tell, I had never met a Christian. At least I had never met anyone who talked about knowing Jesus personally. I poured out my frustrations to my pastor, Malcolm Nygren, whom I had not seen for a long time. His final words were, 'Come to Sunday school. There's a couple you must meet.'

I walked into the class that morning feeling awkward. I wanted solid answers, not pat Sunday school rhetoric. Without knowing it, I took a seat next to the teacher – a tall, dignified woman named Ethel Renwick. She was elegant, bright-eyed, and chock full of energy. Her graciousness put me at ease immediately.

Three questions burned in me. But before I had a

chance to ask them, she answered them – in sequence. And she answered them well. I was spellbound. As I ventured to ask her other questions, she seemed to take genuine delight in them. I was intrigued to realize that this woman, with so vast a knowledge of the world, was yet a convinced Christian.

She began to talk about knowing Jesus – not as an ethic, or a code of laws, but as a *living* Lord. As I watched her, I perceived a radiance and a presence that spoke to my depths. I felt drawn to her in a way I had never experienced with anyone else. Suddenly it dawned on me that this inexplicable attraction I felt was not to her – it was to Christ in her. Christ *must* have risen, I thought, because he is so alive in her! It was my first glimpse of Jesus, and I loved him instantly. My mind and my heart connected. It was true and I knew it. Relief and joy flooded me as I said to God, 'This is it. This really is it. I'm home . . . at last.'

I had just been converted.

That afternoon I drove over to her house and drank in her words as she read Scripture to me. We met together uncounted times in the weeks that followed, reading the Bible and praying. I grew to know her family well. Her husband, Frank, and their three children, George, Margo and Robert, have all played significant roles in my life. From that Sunday morning fifteen years ago until now, a day has not passed when Ethel has not prayed for me. What impressed me then still impresses me. She is a woman who has fallen hopelessly in love with God. She celebrates his world and the gifts he has given us to enjoy. And she respects the way he intends life to be lived. I have never once heard her give a glib answer. She is a model of godly wholeness.

One of five children, Ethel was brought up in Chicago. Her father, Milan Hulbert, was a noted architect and inventor, decorated by eight countries. Her mother,

Olive, was an American brought up in Europe, an artist fluent in five languages. She was the President of Alliance Française and one of only two women outside France ever to receive the French Legion of Honour. The other woman, Madame Curie, was a personal friend.

Prior to the Second World War, Madame Curie came to America to promote the French Red Cross. During her stay, she stood in endless reception lines, always shaking hands with her gloves on. Underneath those gloves were hands badly eaten by radium. But when it came time to say goodbye to Ethel's mother, she took off her gloves to embrace her – a poignant gesture from an otherwise restrained and quiet woman.

Ethel can remember the infectious excitement among the servants and the children whenever special guests came. They would peep over the banister for a glimpse of Sarah Bernhart or Madame Curie.

By training, Ethel was herself more European than American. She spoke only French until she went to school. Each child in the Hulbert family had a governess to take care of practical needs so that the parents could devote extra time to developing their children's minds and forming their values. Ethel remembers her home as a place of great security and love, where discipline was firm, but love stronger.

Dinner time was a cherished event. Everyone dressed for dinner, wearing a coat and tie or a dress. During the meal, her father would introduce a topic and a lively discussion would ensue. Each child was expected to be well-read and conversant, and all opinions were regarded with respect.

The atmosphere in the Hulbert home was one of tremendous curiosity, characterized by a fervour for knowledge and truth and a deep appreciation of other cultures and ways of life. Each member of the family played an instrument, and together they formed a family orchestra, with Olive Hulbert on the harp and Milan Hulbert on the cello.

Life was good and meant to be appreciated. 'Never be afraid of truth,' her father would say. He made it a practice never to punish the children for telling the truth.

The children's manners were impeccable, and their mother taught them that good manners were a reminder that others were important. She instructed them to make life as easy as possible for others. 'Manners are always motivated by thoughtfulness to others – a reminder that we are not the centre of the universe,' she would say.

Ethel's parents were Episcopalians who trained their children in the ways of the church. But it was not their custom to discuss faith and God. They baptized their children, sent them to Sunday school, and taught them to say their prayers. Faith was assumed, not probed.

Two events in Ethel's life proved to have a profound impact on her. The first happened when she was only thirteen years old. A team of physicians in Chicago had examined her father and concluded that he had only six months to live. Ethel remembers the verdict: 'There is nothing medicine can do.' The children were packed off to boarding schools while their parents, following doctors' orders, went to California. Rather than give up all hope of recovery, Milan Hulbert studied nutrition and devised a diet based on whole grains and other natural foods. 'The doctors said it wouldn't help,' Ethel recalled. 'But it did and he lived to a ripe old age.'

While Ethel was at boarding school, her father sent her wheatgerm and bran. 'Sprinkle this stuff on your cereal,' he wrote. His advice hardly seems remarkable today, but it was astonishing for the 1930s. The impact of her father's cure and his determination to eat natural foods was to have far-reaching implications for Ethel's life and ministry.

Another major event in her life took place in 1932. Her

father's view of education, much akin to his pioneer spirit, was that life was meant to be understood and experienced. He wanted his children to see the whole of life – not to perceive it simply through American eyes. To achieve this goal, he encouraged them to travel, to visit different countries, meet the people, study the language, religion, and food. 'While my parents' friends spent enormous amounts of money on elaborate balls for their daughters,' explained Ethel, 'my parents supported us in our endeavours to appreciate and understand the world.'

Mrs Hulbert and her four tall daughters journeyed not once but three times around the world. In those days, travel was fairly primitive and slow, which meant that the five women had ample time to study the various countries and cultures in which they found themselves. Ethel had always been especially interested in philosophy and religion in college. Now she was able to study each religion close up. She was fascinated by what she saw, and she realized, subsequently, that she was searching for God even then.

The five travellers embarked on their journeys prior to the spread of communism and the spread of industrialization to many of the remote regions of the world. They took freighters through tropical isles and travelled on narrow-gauge railways and all manner of motor vehicles across distant landscapes. They sat on elephants as they swayed through the jungles of the deserted city of Rajputan, blazing with vivid colours and reverberating with the cries of the wild peacocks, parrots, and monkeys. Later, the five women booked passages on an onion freighter, which sailed through the South Pacific, stopping at Borneo and the exotic islands of Mindanao, Jolo, Zamboagna, and Iloilo.

Her father's approach to eating made Ethel curious about the food people ate. The most elaborate meal she encountered was hosted by the burgomaster of Brussels and consisted of eight courses, including everything from pâté to ice-cream bombe.

But they ate the simplest and probably the most nutritious meal seated on the ground with a tribal chief of Iloilo, in the Philippines. There were delicious chunks of roast pork, tapioca kneaded in a large wooden trough, bread, fruit, coconut meat from the shell and fresh vegetables steamed over hot rocks. The natives ate only what their forebears had eaten, and seemed strong, healthy, and happy. And they all had sparkling teeth.

But on her return trips, Ethel also saw people who had converted to the Western diet. To her surprise, many of them were not only unhealthy, flabby and surly, but their teeth were rotten as well. These people had no dentists to counteract the damage done by eating sweets and other such foods. Ethel concluded that the culprit was an unnatural diet. She has not changed her mind.

Eventually, Ethel returned to live in America. The first crisis she faced came when she was still a young adult. Like so many others in the Great Depression, her father's business failed, due in part to a dishonest employee. The Hulbert family went from having everything to nothing. Ethel was forced to go to work immediately, managing a hotel in Chicago. Her reaction to the crisis was twofold: 'On the one hand our parents never let us think that money or material things were important. We were taught to value ideas, culture, music and art. So it was not so much a devastation as a challenge. However, up until that time, my life had been fairly sheltered. I trusted people and believed they were good. But this experience forced me to see that people were not inherently good. I learned that I needed to become more astute in my judgment of character. I couldn't trust everyone I met.'

Later, she met a handsome young man by the name of Frank Renwick, her brother's room-mate at military academy. They married after friendship blossomed into courtship while he studied law. Later, they settled in Colorado Springs, where Frank joined a legal firm.

Ethel was satisfied and content. Her marriage was a happy one; her three children were a delight to her. She didn't question God's existence, but neither did she seek him. She sent the children to Sunday school, even though she and Frank never attended church.

One day her eldest child, George, came home from Sunday school and asked, 'Mother, was Jesus really raised from the dead?' George's simple question took her by surprise. She considered herself a Christian, one whose family had placed great importance on truth. But she felt unable to answer this earnest question from her nine-year-old child.

She asked herself, 'Did Jesus rise from the dead or not?' If so, she would admit the truth and proclaim it to others. If not, she would take her children out of Sunday school. She was determined to find the answer. (Fascinating to me, this same question was the one that, years later, was to drive me to her Sunday school class.)

The next Sunday, she attended church and heard a minister ask: 'Did you come here to find Christ? Unless Christ lives in you, you won't find him in a building.' She kept mulling over what he said. 'Christ in you.' But how can Christ be in a person, she pondered?

She discussed her questions with her husband. She and Frank had always been close. If one was interested in a topic then the other wanted to study it as well. They agreed that it was important to find answers. So they searched. They attended church regularly and Ethel began reading books on Christianity. What she read thrilled her.

'I knew the universe was interrelated, interdependent, and integrated. Christianity made sense of the universe by explaining that God was at the centre. All of nature, all of creation obeyed God, except humans who, having their own will and intellect, went their own way and chose not to fit into his plan. For the first time I saw that sin consisted not simply of an isolated act of wrongdoing but of a state of brokenness and separation from God that resulted in our going our own way. I saw that Christ came for the purpose of making us *one* with God. Christ could live in me through his Holy Spirit abiding in me. If I followed Jesus, I could be empowered by God himself to be a part of his whole purpose for the world.

'I was thrilled to discover a system that made sense. I had seen people of other religions clamouring for God's attention. They were so terrified of God that they hung food outside their huts to keep the Devil away. I'd seen fear and superstition. Now I saw that God *wanted* to live in us. He'd sent Jesus to show us the way.'

Privately, she surrendered and accepted Christ. At once, she felt peace and joy at her decision. It wasn't until two weeks later that she realized she had been converted.

In the meantime, Frank had become warden of a new chapel. During coffee time after the chapel service, Ethel spotted three newcomers. She was intrigued to see that they were carrying Bibles. She introduced herself and discovered that they were British – the Reverend David Steele and two friends. The three seemed pleasant enough, and she quickly telephoned her Latvian cook, asking her to set three more places for dinner.

During the meal, the Renwicks learned that their guests worked for the Navigators and were in town only for the summer. As Ethel peppered the three with questions, David Steele opened his Bible, showed her a passage, and said, 'Does this answer it for you?' Instead of giving her his opinion, he gave her God's word, and God's word spoke to her. David Steele's visit confirmed to Ethel that she had indeed become a Christian. Moreover, through them, she had been introduced to the power of the Scriptures.

Ethel spoke freely to her husband about her new faith. He was eager to read what she had. With his keen legal mind and open heart, he, too, was soon convinced and converted. Their three children were, at this time, all under twelve years of age. 'We didn't preach at them,' Ethel says. 'We simply shared our delight and joy in the Lord. Jesus was real in our home. Each child came to know God and love him. When people ask how we did it, I answer honestly that it was the grace of God. Of course we prayed daily for them and tried to live a life worthy of the gospel. But it was God's goodness that brought each one.'

Ethel and Frank were a team. If Ethel spoke to a group by herself, she could always count on Frank's prayers. And Frank could always rely on her prayers. They were immensely involved in one another's lives. They left articles and pamphlets for each other to read. When they were apart they read the same Bible passages or devotional material. And when they were together, they delighted in sharing the details of their day. I recall once helping Ethel prepare an unexpected dinner. We were in a hurry, and I was a bit frantic when Frank began telling her about his day. Putting down her knife, she gave him her undivided attention. Later she confided to me, 'Having dinner on time is only a *thing*, Becky. But Frank is my husband. Never put things ahead of your husband.'

An intriguing aspect of their relationship had to do with the fact that they both had strong wills. Neither hesitated to state a conviction forcefully. Indeed, there is not one member of the Renwick family who could be called passive. A marriage between two strong-willed people can easily lead to frequent conflict. But this was not true of Ethel and Frank Renwick. Neither of them was volatile by nature. But more than that, they seemed to share great oneness of mind and spirit. I remember noticing the slightest frown steal across Ethel's brow one night at dinner. Frank immediately verbalized the problem that Ethel was grappling with. Clearly, he understood what was going on in Ethel's mind.

Despite this mutual understanding, they had their share of problems to work through and lessons to learn. When I asked Ethel for advice about being a good wife while helping to juggle two busy schedules, she replied, 'Be careful of too much busyness for the Lord. You can end up serving the Devil instead of God.' She told me that one of her first mistakes as a young believer was to become involved in so many Christian activities that Frank began to take second place. 'Living by proper priorities isn't a battle that is won once and then forgotten. It involves the daily discipline of reminding oneself who the most important people to serve and love are. You must *choose* your husband each day,' she explained.

David Steele and the Navigators taught the Renwicks how to study the Bible and impressed upon them the value of memorizing Scripture. After meeting David, they signed up immediately for a couples' conference led by a young minister, Dr Richard Halverson (now chaplain to the US Senate). Dick Halverson had a great impact on both of them. He suggested that they become acquainted with International Christian Leadership (the 'Prayer Breakfast' movement). When Ethel attended one of the first Presidential Prayer Breakfasts for women she found herself sitting next to a twinkly-eyed, spunky Dutch woman by the name of Corrie ten Boom. Corrie and she became lifelong friends, and their friendship provided Ethel with ongoing spiritual nurture.

As a new Christian, Ethel could have been tempted to isolate herself from her 'worldly' friends. Wisdom, as well as the desire to see others come to Christ, kept her from making that mistake. Ethel's love for God was so radiant and apparent that her country-club friends soon noticed the change in her. She did not try to sneak the gospel into every conversation or to force it on people. An approach like that was alien to her gracious nature. And she knew that theologically it was wrong. She believed that God was seeking others as he had sought her. She knew she was co-operating with her creator, so she expected him to work. She had been brought up to view the universe as a whole. Now that she was a Christian, she saw that God was to be glorified in all of life – in her love of people, literature, music, ideas – not just in church and Bible studies. And because she was interested in so many things, it gave God the opportunity to be glorified in many things.

A glance around Ethel's apartment says much about the scope of her life. In one corner is a hand-carved elephant table from India. On a bookshelf stands an antique piece of *cloisonné* china, a jade bowl from Nepal, and a Chinese silver box. In the background is an Italian oil-painted, three-panel screen from the 1800s. On one wall hangs an autographed picture of Victor Hugo, a gift from him to her parents. On another wall is a lovely portrait of 'Madame Le Brun', painted by Ethel's mother at the Louvre. On a Peking rug, the coffee table bears books about Chinese art, Quebec, and several early maps. On the sofa lies her latest manuscript on nutrition from a biblical basis – now a foremost passion. One need only look around to see that she is fascinated by all of life: music, literature, the arts, other cultures, nutrition, health and most importantly, faith.

By her example Ethel convinced me that for the sake of Jesus Christ we must be interesting people. If our only interest is the Bible – as marvellous and important as that is – we will find ourselves limited in our ability to relate to others and even to God himself. As Ethel related God to all of life, without imposing but simply exposing what she believed, people noticed. Her love for God was contagious.

Before long, her friends began asking questions about her faith. They even asked if she would help them understand the Bible. Feeling inadequate to the task, she told them, 'I can't teach you the Bible, but I'll show you how to study it and the Bible will teach you!' From the moment of her first encounter with David Steele, she knew that the Bible could speak for itself; it was 'sharper than any two-edged sword'.

So began her first Bible study. She has ministered through Bible studies ever since. 'Many things take place in a Bible study,' she says. 'First, remember that people often come from liberal but nominally religious backgrounds. They are well-educated, and yet often essentially unaware of the gospel of Jesus Christ. So in a Bible study they see who Jesus is, what he is really like, often for the first time. And Jesus is irresistible! Furthermore, the gospel message is spelled out. Sin is explained. They begin to see the thrill of being a Christian as well as the commitment required. As the leader, I learned firsthand that God empowers us with the Holy Spirit for his tasks.'

One by one, nearly every participant in that first Bible study became a Christian. What started as a Bible study for the purpose of evangelism ended up as a Bible study to nurture and disciple new believers.

Her Bible study ministry led to a speaking ministry. Through the Prayer Breakfast movement she spoke to groups across the country. Then she and Frank moved from Colorado to Arizona, where she organized and became chairperson for the Governor's Wife's prayer luncheon, which included 800 women. Simultaneously, she started several new Bible studies, at one time leading as many as five a week.

How did she do it? She simply prayed that God would guide her to the people he was seeking. She had no strategy, other than what God provided.

Both Frank and Ethel led several classes for couples.

And both had a vital ministry in Arizona, leading groups alone as well as together.

Because of her keen interest in food, Ethel wrote a book at that time entitled *A World of Good Cooking*, which was awarded the bronze medal at the International Cook-book Fair in Frankfurt, Germany.

Then Frank was asked to be the director of the Executive Development Center at the University of Illinois. So they moved to Champaign, Illinois, for two years. The reverberation of their ministry there is still being felt. In Champaign they attended a large, mainline Presbyterian church. The Reverend Malcolm Nygren, the pastor who baptized me and performed my wedding and who has a unique gift for incorporating and using the gifts of others, welcomed the Renwicks warmly.

Both of them taught adult Sunday school classes, in which many, including myself, were converted. They led Bible studies and taught us how to study Scripture on our own. I can remember Ethel saying as I was preparing for my first year of college: 'Now it's your turn to lead a Bible study, Becky.' I gulped, but her suggestion that I pray about it inspired me to be on the lookout for the people God would give me.

The Renwicks believed that most evangelicals tend to flock to the same church, often leaving more liberal congregations devoid of vibrant, committed evangelicals. They themselves found mainline churches full of open and spiritually hungry people. Ethel told of one example: 'I recall meeting a woman for lunch who was a pillar of the church. We talked about programmes and organizational details. But on the way home, she began pouring out her personal problems. After we had discussed them, I simply said, "Let's pray about this. The Lord cares so much about you. He'll show us the way for you." She looked at me in stunned silence, then said, "No one has ever prayed for me before." The woman began to weep. She had gone to church all her life, yet she had never realized that Jesus was alive and personal, that Christ could live in us and love us and guide us.'

'If only Christians could see the power they have in the Holy Spirit,' Ethel says. 'We are small and weak. But God himself lives in us! And he will multiply what we do. We may be only one small pebble in a pond, but that one plunk of obedience causes motion in the rest of the water. God multiplies what we do!'

Hazel Offner, a woman who has shaped my life and has had a profound impact through her Bible study leadership in the Champaign-Urbana area, says of Ethel: 'I have never met anyone who so stretched my vision. Together, we drew up a chart of my neighbourhood and prayed for each family by name. We wrote down the names of people in the Presbyterian church whom Ethel had just met and prayed for them. Ethel had never met my neighbours, and I had never met her Presbyterian friends, but, together, we believed God could accomplish great things in them and in us as we prayed. The result for me was a neighbourhood Bible study which turned into an all-community study of forty-five small groups. My life – and my understanding of God – was never the same again.

'Ethel's faith was contagious. There wasn't any dream too big for her to dream and to believe that God would cause to become reality. She knew that there was marvellous untapped potential in everyone around her, and she was so expectant – both before God in prayer and demonstrably to the persons themselves as her soul touched theirs – that it was impossible not to catch her faith and her vision and to become expectant too. She seldom expressed negative feelings; rather, there was constant, pervasive expectancy that God was just waiting and was eager to change and use people. I can recall several times when a name would come to her as we were talking and she would interrupt the conversation for a moment and spontaneously lift that person to God. By the time she left Champaign, after two years there, one life after another had been deeply affected and changed by God.'

When Ethel and Frank returned to Arizona, where she now lives, she worked at the International Food Bazaar, managing fourteen kitchens representing nine different nationalities. Her knowledge of international cuisines stood her in good stead – and so did her knowledge of people. 'Waitresses and waiters would ask me if we could talk. They told me they were addicted to drugs and wanted to stop. They asked for my help.' Ethel would listen intently to convey a genuine concern as well as God's love for each person. She also invited a guest speaker, a doctor, to lecture to the entire staff on why drugs led only to a dead end. And she regularly scheduled Christian speakers who had been on drugs themselves to come and speak to the staff on various subjects, including faith in Christ.

As she recounted this story, I marvelled at the thought of teenagers admitting such a problem to their boss. After all, she could have sacked them. But they sensed that they could trust her. Such trust says a great deal about Ethel, but she insists that it says much more about God. 'It's Jesus in me that enabled me to see pain I might otherwise have missed. He gives us a love that truly comes from above. If you'd told me in college that I would love a drug addict – much less know one – I would have been amazed. But when God lives in you, what draws you into people's lives isn't duty or social work, it's his love that keeps penetrating the barrier.'

Part of her sensitivity to pain comes from the presence of God in her life and part comes from firsthand experience. Throughout the years, her life has been marked by pain as well as privilege.

Several of her close friends have suffered from

alcoholism. She has cleaned up after them, held them and provided hour-to-hour emotional support as well as physical nurture. She has had the painful experience of telling some that they were addicted to alcohol and needed professional help, only to be avoided by them from that time on.

Her own family suffered tragic car accidents, serious physical problems and other crushing blows, resulting in the premature deaths of three of her five brothers and sisters. Perhaps her deepest grief has been over the death of her husband Frank.

In a way that only God could order, I was at home one night, contrary to my previous expectations, when George Renwick called me with the sad news that his father was gravely ill. Abruptly, George said, 'Becky, call mother, right now, please.' I hung up, dialled, and Ethel answered, having been informed only seconds before that her husband had died.

Later, she said, 'There are so many stages one goes through with the death of a spouse. At first, I felt that half of me had died. My major human support was buried. Nothing else seemed to matter. I felt I had no place, no mooring, apart from the constancy of God's love and the comfort of my children. Six months later the phone would ring, and I would begin immediately to recount in my mind all that I wanted to tell Frank. As I leapt to the receiver, I would remember that he was gone. It's hard to describe just how deeply the loss of someone you love can affect you. But as I received God's love, as well as the tremendous care of my children and friends, I began to be healed. The numbness started to leave.'

One of the friends to offer comfort was Corrie ten Boom. It was a remarkable experience for me to sit in a living room with Ethel, her sister Adele, her three children and Corrie. It was obvious that Corrie loved Ethel and knew only too well the pain that comes from the death of a loved one. But her eyes shone as she said in her heavy Dutch accent, 'My dear sister, vee don't vant him back. Frank ist vith our Jesus now! *Think* of it.'

After the initial pain, Ethel experienced yet another level of grief. 'I had to deal with my new social status. People treated me differently as a widow. I was no longer invited to all the social gatherings that I had been. Businesses did not take me as seriously. A male voice on the telephone carries more clout, I discovered, than a female voice. So I had to learn to deal with that.

'The third, unexpected stage of recovery happened when God gave me a new ministry. My book on nutrition *Let's Eat Real Food* was published in 1977 and is now in its eighth edition. I began leading seminars for individual Christians as well as for schools and secular groups, teaching others how to eat sensibly and responsibly. After that, all kinds of opportunities opened up.'

All kinds of opportunities, indeed! One week before I flew to Arizona to interview her, I was speaking at a conference in Pennsylvania. As I was autographing books, a woman came up to me and said, 'I couldn't believe you mentioned Ethel Renwick in the foreword to your book. She changed your life spiritually and my life physically. My family suffered from headaches, hypoglycaemia and poor eating habits. Reading her book changed our eating patterns. We feel like new people. We keep her book on our coffee table and have given copies to our friends.'

In short, there is life after tragedy and loss. 'Sorrow,' relates Ethel, 'is God's greatest opportunity to deal with us. Because in those times we are so defenceless. We know that we simply cannot continue on our own. We can't heal ourselves or fill the gap. But God can meet us on our knees. He can have deeper access to us in our pain. And he does heal the brokenhearted and bind up their wounds.'

What exactly is her present ministry? 'In many ways, I

believe God has taken all the strands of my life and made them come together, to do what he called me to now,' she says.

Perhaps a story will best illustrate. I told the Lord as I fell asleep in Ethel's apartment on the night of my interview with her that I wanted to convey the depth and significance of what she does. I was awakened early the next morning by a telephone call for Ethel. It was from a woman who had recently brought a friend to see Ethel. The friend had attempted suicide twice. Ethel had spent four hours listening to her spill out her problems. Ethel asked her spiritual questions, but she also inquired about her eating and drinking habits. It became clear that in addition to being emotionally and spiritually troubled, she was also a physical wreck. She was living on soft drinks and valium.

So Ethel suggested that this young woman change her eating patterns and begin filling her body with nutritious foods. She told her that God cared for her physically and emotionally as well as spiritually. If she wanted real health, in every dimension, she needed to be invaded by God through Jesus Christ. It was clear that the distraught woman was moved, almost astonished by the kind of God who loved every part of her. She had never heard the gospel presented in such an integrated way. She thought Christianity was just for the soul. She had not realized that God made provision for every dimension of life – body and soul. He wanted her to be whole and she knew she was fragmented. She left, saying she was determined to change her physical habits and to seek God as well.

That morning's telephone call related the news that the troubled woman was on the road to physical recovery and spiritual renewal. For the first time, she felt hope and not despair. Ironically, the person telephoning with the good news had herself gone to Ethel only months before with many of the same problems: feeling suicidal and addicted to valium. Through Ethel's help she too rededicated her life to Jesus Christ.

Says Ethel: 'We say we're concerned about wholeness as Christians, yet we so often avoid the physical dimension. The only thing that nourishes the brain and the nervous system is food. Yet it never occurs to us to check what a depressed person has been eating, as one indication of the source of the problem. Food affects how we see the world. It can make our minds clear or fuzzy. If we load our bodies with sugar and caffeine, we get a lift only to crash later. How can we be a vital witness to God? God wants his children to be strong and healthy and clear-minded – not addicts.'

How did Ethel's ministry come to include a concern for people's physical well-being? 'It was because I kept meeting people who didn't feel well. It was especially alarming how many of them were Christians who told me they were tired, with little energy and feeling depressed.' They often felt the culprit was spiritual inadequacy. As Ethel questioned them about their diet she was disheartened by how poorly they ate. They cared deeply about the Kingdom, yet they ignored and even abused the vessel God works through to build his Kingdom – our bodies.

In our Western diet, Ethel warns, 'we eat more sweets than eggs, more sugar than vegetables, fruits and eggs combined; we drink more soft drinks than milk. And since 1971, we eat more processed foods than fresh foods. We send our children off to school carrying a lunch box filled with a sandwich made of fluffy enriched white bread, potato crisps and a couple of biscuits, not even stopping to think what ingredients or chemicals are in those basic items. We often reward children with destructive food, and then we wonder why they seem so highly-strung and irritable. We have cake sales at church to raise money for the poor by selling impoverished, nutrient-less food.'

Strong words? Then hear what she has to say about Christians! 'The Lord recently sent me someone who loves him, a pastor's wife, who was in great need. Her story is the same I hear from so many – unexplained anxiety, depression, fatigue, increased mental problems. The doctors, after many tests, found nothing wrong with her. Yet her diet was atrocious (but very usual).'

Ethel believes that our ignorance of today's food has serious consequences and that Christians are especially accountable for these consequences. Her latest book, *Feeding the Faithful*, rises out of just this conviction. In the book she writes:

> There has been a radical departure in many ways from the food which God designed for our bodies and the food we accept today with little question. . . . Perhaps one reason that scripture mentions eating and drinking to the glory of God is because, when we disobey this, we self-destruct to some degree; we are less than we could be for Him.

The strands have, indeed, come together – personal commitment to Christ, energetic witness in the world, the understanding of the relationship between physical and spiritual well-being. Through her life, Ethel has provided an example of tireless dedication and caring love to countless individuals. Hers is an example that merits close examination.

The underlying assumption of this book is that in addition to needing heroes and role-models we must be those things for others.

Ours is a strange age. Never have we hungered more for heroes or tried so hard to defame them. We still ache for heroes, even if we are no longer comfortable with them. Pete Dawkins, all-American football player, Rhodes scholar, the most luminous graduate of West Point and now, aged forty-three, the youngest general in the US Army, said in an interview with my husband, Wesley, 'A lot of things that are central parts of our lives are transcendent or abstract. But it's hard for us to deal with courage or dedication or sacrifice in the abstract. We need to have people who embody those qualities, who are reassuring and real. What we really want is to believe in people.' Yet we live in an age of the 'anti-hero'. As Dawkins says, 'We seem to turn on ours [heroes] with special fervour, driven by an almost compulsive need to scratch and rub anyone of heroic dimension until we find a wart or flaw. We microscopically examine people in public life until we find something about them that is flawed.'

Yet the human heart cannot seem to resist the desire to elevate someone above the masses: whether this tendency is realized in the exuberant outpouring of joy and enthusiasm for the Pope, the poignant scene where hundreds kept vigil outside Yoko Ono's home the night John Lennon was killed, or the wearing of hideous T-shirts advertising heavy-metal bands. As disparate as these examples are, we must listen to what our culture is telling us. We need heroes. People want to believe in someone.

We must distinguish between *celebrities* and *heroes.* Never be ashamed of having a hero or of being one. But be wary of the celebrity-mania that exists today. There will always be an abundance of celebrities, but there is a paucity of genuine heroes in the land.

Garry Trudeau, the creator of the comic strip 'Doonesbury', spoke of this in 1981: 'This is a deeply cynical age where generosity is in short supply. You will find that this technological society will soon reveal its limitations. It is a world where taking a stand has come to mean finding the nearest trap door for escape. . . . You will find that your worth is measured not by what you are, but by how you are perceived. There is something disturbing in our society when men wish not to be esteemed, but to be envied. . . . When that happens, God help us.'

A popular television show was being broadcast in Washington, just the kind of thing that city loves best: top news men and women questioning a news-making political celebrity. Senator Barry Goldwater was an exceptionally good guest that night. His answers were characteristically tough, feisty, and candid. As the programme came to a close, one interviewer said, 'We always ask this, sir, in the last thirty seconds, realizing it's not nearly as significant as the other things we've discussed, but who has been the greatest influence in your life? Who has been one of your heroes?' There was silence. One by one each reporter looked up. The silence became awkward. The camera zoomed in for a close-up and the reason for the silence became immediately apparent. Senator Goldwater was fighting back his emotions. His voice breaking, he apologized to the startled reporters.

Finally he said, 'It's a man you've probably never heard of. I'm sure he himself had no idea of the impact he made on me as a young man. But he was my role-model for all the things I've ever aspired to be. He pointed me in the right direction. He believed in me and he cared for me. He was a great man.'

That night a politically powerful man wept publicly on television. Not because he had won an election, or lost an election, or was indicted (as is too often the case). He wept because he had a hero. That night I realized that Senator Goldwater and I have a great deal in common. The thought of my hero also makes me weep.

Martyn Lloyd-Jones

by J. I. Packer

David Martyn Lloyd-Jones, the 'Doctor' as he was called in public by all who knew him (even his wife!), resigned in 1968 after thirty years as pastor of London's Westminster Chapel. He died on St David's Day, 1 March, 1981. He was the greatest man I have ever known, and I am sure that there is more of him under my skin than there is of any other of my human teachers. I do not mean that I ever thought of myself as his pupil, nor did he ever see himself as my instructor; what I gained from him came by spiritual osmosis, if the work of the Holy Spirit can be so described. When we met and worked together, as we did fairly regularly for over twenty years, we were colleagues, senior and junior, linked in a brotherhood of endeavour that for the most part overrode a quarter of a century's difference in our ages.

It was a shared concern that first brought us together: I, who did not know him, went with a friend who did in order to ask if he, as a Puritan enthusiast, would host and chair a conference that we hoped to organize on Puritan theology. He did so, and the conference became an annual event. Other shared concerns – explaining evangelicalism to the British Council of Churches; the now-defunct *Evangelical Magazine*; Reformed fellowships and preaching meetings; the quest for revival – these kept us together from 1949 to 1970.

For me it was an incalculably enriching relationship. To be wholly forthcoming, genial, warmhearted, confidential, sympathetic and supportive to ministerial colleagues of all ages was part of the Doctor's greatness. It was, I think, a combined expression of his Presbyterian clericalism, based on the parity of all clergy, plus his feelings as a physician for the common dignity of all who have charge of others' welfare, plus the expansive informality of the Welsh family head. It was an attitude that left countless ministers feeling like a million dollars – significant in their calling, purposeful about it and invigorated for it. The Doctor's magnetic blend of clarity, certainty, common sense and confidence in God made him a marvellous encourager, as well as a great moulder of minds. He was a pastor of pastors *par excellence*. He would have hated to be called a bishop, but no-one ever fulfilled towards clergy a more truly episcopal ministry. I know that much of my vision today is what it is because he was what he was, and his influence has no doubt gone deeper than I can trace.

To be sure, we did not always see eye to eye. Over questions of the church's responsibility we were never on the same wavelength, and this led eventually to a parting of the ways. Ironically, what made our head-on collision possible was the convictions we had in common, which for many years had bound us together and distinguished us from many, if not most, of England's evangelicals. What these convictions added up to was a consuming concern for the church as a product and expression of the gospel. We both saw the centrality of the church in God's plan of grace. Both of us believed in the crucial importance of the local congregation as the place of God's presence, the agent of his purposes, and the instrument of his praise. We both sought the church's spiritual unity, internal and external – that is, oneness of evangelical faith and life, appearing in a unanimous Bible-based confession and a challenging Spirit-wrought sanctity. Both of us sought the church's purity – the elimination of false doctrine, unworthy worship and lax living. We both backed interdenominational evangelical activities, not as an ideal form of Christian unity, but as a regrettable necessity due to the inaction of the churches themselves, which made it certain that if para-church bodies did not do this or that job it would never get done at all. Had these convictions not been so central to both our identities, we should not have clashed as we did.

The possibility of an explosion was there from the start. I was English and Anglican and the Doctor a Welsh chapel-man to his fingertips. He had little respect for Englishness, or for Anglicanism as a heritage or Anglicans as a tribe. (He saw the English as pragmatists, lacking principle, and Anglicans as formalists, lacking theology. When he told me that I was not a true Anglican he meant it as a compliment.) His world was that of seventeenth-century Puritans, eighteenth-century evangelicals and nineteenth-century Welsh Calvinists. It was a world of bare chapel walls and extended extempore prayer; of preachers as prophets and community leaders; of spiritual conversions, conflicts, griefs and joys touching the deep heart's core; of the quest for power in preaching as God's ordinary means of enlivening his people; and of separation to start new assemblies if truth was being throttled in the old ones. In all of this the

Doctor was a precise counterpart of the Baptist minister C. H. Spurgeon, who himself fulfilled an awesome ministry of a Puritan evangelical type in London nearly a century earlier. The only difference was that Spurgeon learned his nonconformity not in Wales but in East Anglia. I never heard the Doctor described as Spurgeon *redivivus*, but the description would have fitted. Like Spurgeon, he thought Anglicanism discredited and hopeless. To look for genuine, widespread evangelical renewal in the Church of England seemed to him 'mid-summer madness' (his phrase), and he was sure that in doing this I was wasting my time. 'They won't accept you,' he used to tell me, and it was plain that he hoped eventually to see me leave the Anglican fold.

Denominationalism finally became the breaking-point. Officially a minister of the Presbyterian Church of Wales, the Doctor had become a convinced Independent, viewing each congregation as a wholly self-determining unit under Christ, in the Spirit and before God. In the 1960s he began to voice a vision of a new fellowship of evangelical clergy and congregations in England that would have no links with 'doctrinally mixed' denominations, that is, the Church of England, the English Methodist Church and the English Baptist Union. To winkle evangelicals out of these bodies he invoked the principle of secondary separation, maintaining that evangelicals not only were free to leave such denominations but must do so, for they were guilty by association of all the errors of those from whom they did not cut themselves off ecclesiastically. Opposing and repudiating those errors, so he urged, does not clear one of guilt unless one actually withdraws. Because my public actions showed that I disagreed with all this and remained a reforming Anglican despite it, our work together ceased in 1970.

The Doctor believed that his summons to separation

was a call for evangelical unity as such, and that he was not a denominationalist in any sense. In continuing to combat error, commend truth and strengthen evangelical ministry as best I could in the Church of England, he thought I was showing myself a denominationalist and obstructing evangelical unity, besides being caught in a hopelessly compromised position. By contrast, I believed that the claims of evangelical unity do not require ecclesiastical separation where the faith is not actually being denied and renewal remains possible; that the action for which the Doctor called would be, in effect, the founding of a new, loose-knit, professedly undenominational denomination; and that he, rather than I, was the denominationalist for insisting that evangelicals must all belong to this new grouping and no other. His claim that this was what the times and the truth required did not convince me. Was either of us right? History will judge, and to history I remit the matter.

Born and reared in South Wales, he was fourteen in 1914 when his family moved to London. He entered the medical school of St Bartholomew's Hospital at the early age of sixteen, graduated brilliantly in 1921, and soon became chief clinical assistant to his former teacher, the Royal Physician, Sir Thomas (later, Lord) Horder, an outstanding diagnostician whose analytical habit of mind reinforced his own. But he soon found that medical practice did not satisfy him, since it centred on the body while the deepest problems are in the soul. Having found his own way to an assurance of God's pardoning mercy towards him, he became sure that God was calling him to preach the gospel to others. By 'gospel' he meant the old-fashioned, Bible-based, life-transforming message of radical sin in every human heart and radical salvation through faith in Christ alone – a definite message quite distinct from the indefinite hints and euphoric vaguenesses that to his mind had usurped the gospel's place in most British pulpits. In 1927, having decided that seminary training was not for him, he became lay pastor of the Forward Movement Mission Church of the Presbyterian (Calvinistic Methodist) Church of Wales in Sandfields, Aberavon, not far from Swansea. On his first Sunday as pastor he called for spiritual reality in terms so characteristic of his subsequent ministry that it is worth quoting his words at length.

> Young men and women, my one great attempt here at Aberavon, as long as God gives me strength to do so, will be to try to prove to you not merely that Christianity is reasonable, but that ultimately, faced as we all are at some time or other with the stupendous fact of life and death, nothing else is reasonable. That is, as I see it, the challenge of the gospel of Christ to the modern world. My thesis will ever be, that, face to face with the deeper questions of life and death, all our knowledge and our culture will fail us, and that our only hope of peace is to be found in the crucified Christ. . . . My request is this: that we all be honest with one another in our conversation and discussions. . . . Do let us be honest with one another and never profess to believe more than is actually true to our experience. Let us always, with the help of the Holy Spirit, testify to our belief, *in full*, but never a word more. . . . I do not know what your experience is, my friends, but as for myself, I shall feel much more ashamed to all eternity for the occasions on which I said I believed in Christ when in fact I did not, than for the

occasions when I said honestly that I could not truthfully say that I did believe. If the church of Christ on earth could but get rid of the parasites who only believe that they ought to believe in Christ, she would, I am certain, count once more in the world as she did in her early days, and as she has always done during times of spiritual awakening. I ask you therefore tonight, and shall go on asking you and myself, the same question: Do you know what you know about the gospel? Do you question yourself about your belief and make sure of yourself?*

'Prove', 'reasonable', 'modern world', 'honest', 'the crucified Christ', 'the help of the Holy Spirit', 'experience', 'spiritual awakening', 'question yourself' – these were keynote terms and phrases in the Doctor's preaching, first to last. He started as he meant to go on, and as he did in fact go on, seeing himself as an evangelist first and foremost and seeking constantly the conversion and quickening of folk in the churches who thought they were Christians already.

Though the Sandfields ministry was directed to working-class people, the intellectual challenge was always at its forefront. Social activities were scrapped, and with intense seriousness the Doctor gave himself to preaching and teaching the word of God. Soon he was ordained. The congregation grew, many conversions occurred, the church was admired as a model and its minister was the best-known preacher in Wales.

In 1938 the Doctor moved to London's Congregational 'cathedral', Westminster Chapel, as colleague to the veteran G. Campbell Morgan. There, after Morgan's

*I. H. Murray, *David Martyn Lloyd-Jones: The First Forty Years, 1899–1939* (Edinburgh: Banner of Truth Trust, 1982), pp. 135 ff.

retirement in 1943, he was sole pastor for a quarter of a century, preaching morning and evening every Sunday except for his annual holidays in July and August. As in Wales, he lived at full stretch. Guest preaching during the first part of the week and pastoral counselling by appointment were regular parts of his life. On each Friday night he taught publicly at the Chapel, for several years by discussion, then by doctrinal lectures, and for the last twelve years by exposition of Paul's letter to the Romans. At both Sunday services, and on the Friday nights when Romans was explored, attendance was regularly nearer two thousand than one. In addition to his steady converting and nurturing ministry there, he exercised much influence on English evangelicalism as a whole.

He did a great deal to guide, stabilize, and deepen the evangelical student work of the young Inter-Varsity Fellowship of Evangelical Unions (IVF, now UCCF). At first he hesitated to touch IVF, for he was Welsh, middle-class, church-orientated, and intellectually and theologically alert, whereas IVF was a loose interdenominational grouping that had grown out of children's and teenagers' ministry and was characterized by what the Doctor saw as brainless English upper-class pietism. But in partnership with another ex-medical man, the quiet genius Douglas Johnson, he fulfilled a leadership role in IVF for twenty years, and did more than anyone to give the movement its present temper of intellectual concern, confidence and competence.

In due course the International Fellowship of Evangelical Students (IFES) was formed, an umbrella organization uniting student-led movements of the IVF type all round the world. The Doctor drew up its basis, defined its platform, chaired its meetings for the first twelve years and continued in association with it, first as president and then as vice-president, to the end of his life. In this, too, he was closely linked with the self-effacing Johnson, whose behind-the-scenes activity was a major factor in bringing IFES to birth.

Throughout his London years, the Doctor was also host and chairman of the Westminster Ministers' Fraternal (the Westminster Fellowship, as it was called), which met monthly at the Chapel for a day of discussion and mutual encouragement. Originally an idea of Johnson's, the Fraternal grew to a membership of 400 in the early 1960s. Through his masterful leadership of it, the Doctor focused its vision and shaped the ideals of many evangelical clergy in all denominations.

He campaigned steadily for the study of older evangelical literature, particularly the Puritans, Jonathan Edwards and eighteenth- and nineteenth-century biography, from which he had himself profited enormously. Also, he gave much support to the Banner of Truth Trust, a publishing house specializing in reprints, which was formed and financed from within his congregation. It can safely be said that the current widespread appreciation in Britain of older evangelical literature owes more to him than to anyone.

What a fascinating human being he was! Slightly built, with a great domed cranium, head thrust forward, a fighter's chin and a grim line to his mouth, he radiated resolution, determination, and an unwillingness to wait for ever. A very strong man, you would say, and you would be right. You can sense this from any photograph of him, for he never smiled into the camera. There was a touch of the old-fashioned about him: he wore linen collars, three-piece suits and boots in public, spoke on occasion of crossing-sweepers and washerwomen and led worship as worship was led a hundred years before his time. In the pulpit he was a lion, fierce on matters of principle, austere in his gravity, able in his prime both to growl and to roar as his argument required. Informally, however, he was a delightfully relaxed person, superb company, twinkling and witty to the last degree. His wit was as astringent as it was quick and could leave you feeling you had been licked by a cow. His answer to the question, posed in a ministers' meeting, 'Why are there so few men in our churches?' was: 'Because there are so many old women in our pulpits!' In 1952 he complained to me of the presence at the Puritan conference of two young ladies from his congregation. 'They're only here for the men!' said he. 'Well, Doctor,' I replied, 'as a matter of fact I'm going to marry one of them.' (I had proposed and been accepted the night before.) I thought that would throw him, but it didn't at all. Quick as a flash came the answer, 'Well, you see I was right about one of them; now what about the other?' There's repartee for you!

He did not suffer fools gladly and had a hundred ways of deflating pomposity. Honest, diffident people, however, found in him a warmth and friendliness that amazed them.

For he was a saint, a holy man of God: a naturally proud person whom God made humble; a naturally quick-tempered person whom God taught patience; a naturally contentious person to whom God gave restraint and wisdom; a natural egoist, conscious of his own great ability, whom God set free from self-seeking to serve the servants of God. In his natural blend of intelligence with arrogance, quickness with dogmatism, and geniality with egocentricity, he was like two other small men who also wanted to see things changed, and spent their mature years changing them. The first, John Wesley, another great leader and encourager, just as shrewd and determined as the Doctor though less well focused theologically, shaped a new, passionate style of piety for over a hundred thousand Englishmen in his own lifetime. The second, Richard Wagner, not a Christian, but a magnetic, emotional, commanding personality, charming, ingenious, well aware of his own powers, and very articulate (though muddily; not like the Doctor!), changed the course of Western music. The Doctor might not have appreciated either of these comparisons, but I think they are both in point. It is fascinating to observe what sort of goodness it is that each good man exhibits, and to try to see where it has come from. The Doctor was an intellectual like John Calvin, and like him said little about his inward experiences with God, but as with Calvin the moral effects of grace in his life were plain to see. His goodness, like Calvin's, had been distilled out of the raw material of a temperament inclined to pride, sharpness and passion. Under the power of gospel truth, those inclinations had been largely mortified and replaced by habits of humility, goodwill and self-control. In public discussion he could be severe to the point of crushing, but always with transparent patience and good humour. I think he had a temper, but I never saw him lose it, though I saw stupid people 'take him on' in discussion and provoke him in a manner almost beyond belief. His self-control was marvellous: only the grace of God suffices to explain it.

Beyond all question, the Doctor was brilliant: he had a mind like a razor, an almost infallible memory, staggering speed of thought and total clarity and ease of speech, no matter what the subject or how new the notions he was voicing. His thinking always seemed to be far ahead of yours; he could run rings round anyone in debate; and it was hard not to treat him as an infallible oracle. However, a clever man only becomes a great one if two further qualities are added to his brilliance, namely, nobility of purpose and some real personal force in pursuing it. The Doctor manifested both these further qualities in an outstanding way.

He was essentially a preacher, and as a preacher primarily an evangelist. Some might question this since most of his twenty books (edited sermons, every one of them) have a nurturing thrust, and the quickening of Christians and churches was certainly the main burden of his final years of ministry. Also, his was supremely what Spurgeon called an 'all-round' ministry, in practice as rich pastorally as it was evangelistically. But no-one who ever heard him preach the gospel from the Gospels and show how it speaks to the aches and follies and nightmares of the modern heart will doubt that this was where his own focus lay, and where as a communicator he was at his finest. He was bold enough to believe that because inspired preaching changes individuals it can change the church and thereby change the world; and the noble purpose of furthering such change was the whole of his life's agenda. As for force in pursuing his goal, the personal electricity of his pulpit communication was unique. All his energy went into his preaching: not only animal energy, of which he had a good deal, but also the God-given liveliness and authority that in past eras was called 'unction'. He effectively proclaimed the greatness of God, and of Christ, and of the soul, and of eternity, and supremely of saving grace – the everlasting gospel, old yet ever new, familiar yet endlessly wonderful.

'Unction' is the anointing of God's Holy Spirit upon the preacher in and for his act of opening up God's written word. George Whitefield, who was in his own day the undisputed front-man of the evangelical awakening on both sides of the Atlantic, and whom the Doctor confessedly took as a role-model, once in conversation gave a printer *carte blanche* to transcribe and publish his sermons provided that he printed 'the thunder and the lightning too' – but who could do that? In the same way there was in the Doctor's preaching thunder and lightning that no tape or transcription ever did or could capture – power, I mean, to mediate a realization of God's presence (for when Whitefield spoke of thunder and lightning he was talking biblically, not histrionically, and so am I). Nearly forty years on, it still seems to me that all I have ever known about preaching was given me in the winter of 1948–49, when I worshipped at Westminster Chapel with some regularity. Through the thunder and lightning, I felt and saw as never before the glory of Christ and his gospel as modern man's only lifeline, and learned by experience why historic Protestantism looks on preaching as the supreme means of grace and of communion with God. Preaching, thus viewed and valued, was the centre of the Doctor's life: into it he poured himself unstintingly; for it he pleaded untiringly. Rightly, he believed that preachers are born rather than made, and that preaching is caught more than it is taught, and that the best way to vindicate preaching is to preach. And preach he did, almost greedily, till the very end of his life – 'this our short, uncertain life and earthly pilgrimage', as by constant repetition in his benedictions he had taught Christians to call it.

I mentioned thunder and lightning: that could give a wrong impression. Pulpit dramatics and rhetorical rhapsodies the Doctor despised and never indulged in; his concern was always with the flow of thought, and the emotion he expressed as he talked was simply the outward sign of passionate thinking. The style is the man, 'the physiognomy of the mind', as Schopenhauer rather portentously said, and this was supremely true of the Doctor. He never put on any sort of act, but talked in exactly the same way from the pulpit, the lecture-desk or the armchair, treating all without exception as fellow enquirers after truth, who might or might not be behaving in character at just that moment. Always he spoke as a debater making a case (the Welsh are great debaters); as a physician making a diagnosis; as a theologian, blessed with what he once recognized in another as a 'naturally theological mind', thinking things out from Scripture in terms of God; and as a man who loved history and its characters and had thought his way into the minds and motives, the insights and the follies, of very many of them.

He had read widely, thought deeply and observed a great deal of human life with a clear and clinical eye, and as he was endlessly interested in his fellow-men, so he was a fascinating well of wisdom whenever he talked. When he preached, he usually eschewed the humour which bubbled out of him so naturally at other times and concentrated on serious, down-to-earth, educational exposition. He planned and paced his discourses (three-quarters of an hour or more) with evident care, never letting the argument move too fast for the ordinary listener and sometimes, in fact, working so hard in his first few minutes to engage his hearers' minds that he had difficulty getting the argument under way at all. But his preaching always took the form of an argument, biblical, evangelical, doctrinal and spiritual, starting most usually with the foolishness of human self-sufficiency, as expressed in some commonly held opinions and policies, moving to what may be called the Isaianic inversion whereby man who thinks himself great is shown to be small and God whom he treats as small is shown to be great, and always closing within sight of Christ – his cross and his grace. In his prime, when he came to the Isaianic inversion and the awesome and magnificent thing that he had to declare at that point about our glorious, self-vindicating God, the Doctor would let loose the thunder and lightning with a spiritual impact that was simply stunning. I have never known anyone whose speech communicated such a sense of the reality of God as did the Doctor in those occasional moments of emphasis and doxology. Most of the time, however, it was clear, steady analysis, reflection, correction and instruction, based on simple thoughts culled from the text, set out in good order with the minimum of extraneous illustration or decoration. He knew that God's way to the heart is through the mind (he often insisted that the first thing the gospel does to a man is to make him think), and he preached in a way designed to help people think and thereby grasp truth – and in the process be grasped by it, and so be grasped by the God whose truth it is.

A Welshman who inspired Englishmen, as David Lloyd-George once did on the political front; an eighteenth-century man (so he called himself) with his finger firmly on mid-twentieth century pulses; a preacher who could make 'the old, old story of Jesus and his love' sound so momentously new that you felt you had never heard it before; a magisterial pastor and theologian whose only degrees were his medical qualifications; an erudite intellectual who always talked the language of the common man; a 'Bible Calvinist' (as distinct from a 'system Calvinist': his phrase again) whose teaching all evangelicals could and did applaud; an evangelical who resolutely stood apart from the evangelical establishment, challenging its shallowness and short-sightedness constantly; a spiritual giant, just over five feet tall; throwback and prophet; loner and communicator; a compound of combative geniality, wisdom, and vision, plus a few endearing quirks – the Doctor was completely his own man, and quite unique.

On 6 February, 1977, the fiftieth anniversary of the start of his ministry at Sandfields, the Doctor returned and preached. He announced as his text 1 Corinthians 2:2, 'For I determined not to know any thing among you, save Jesus Christ, and him crucified.' His sermon, printed in the *Evangelical Magazine of Wales*, in April 1981, the first issue following his death, began as follows:

I have a number of reasons for calling your attention tonight to this particular statement. One of them – and I think you will forgive me for it – is that it was actually the text I preached on, on the first Sunday night I ever visited this Church . . .

I call attention to it not merely for that reason, but rather because it is still my determination, it is still what I am endeavouring, as God helps me, to do. I preached on this text then – I have no idea what I said in detail, I have not got the notes – but I did so because it was an expression of my whole attitude towards life. It was what I felt was the commission that had been given to me. And I call attention to it again because it is still the same, and because I am profoundly convinced that this is what should control our every endeavour as Christian people and as members of the Christian Church at this present time.

There followed a very clear exposition of salvation through the atoning death of Jesus Christ, and then from the 77-year-old preacher came the application:

Men and women, is Jesus Christ and him crucified everything to you? This is the question. It is a personal matter. Is he central? Does he come before anything and everything? Do you pin your faith in him and in him alone? Nothing else works. He works! I stand here because I can testify to the same thing. 'E'er since, by faith, I saw the stream/Thy flowing wounds supply,/Redeeming love has been my theme,/And shall be till I die.' 'God forbid that I should glory, save in the cross of our Lord

> Jesus Christ, by whom the world is crucified unto me, and I [crucified] unto the world' (Gal. 6:14).
>
> My dear friends, in the midst of life we are in death. This is not theory; this is personal, this is practical. How are you living? Are you happy? Are you satisfied? How do you face the future? Are you alarmed? Terrified? How do you face death? You have got to die. . . . What will you have when that end comes? You will have nothing, unless you have Jesus Christ and him crucified. . . . do you know him? Have you believed in him? Do you see that he alone can avail you in life, in death and to all eternity? If not, make certain tonight. Fall at his feet. He will receive you, and he will make you a new man or a new woman. He will give you a new life. He will wash you. He will cleanse you. He will renovate you. He will regenerate you and you will become a saint, and you will follow after that glorious company of saints that have left this very place and are now basking in the sunshine of his face in the glory everlasting. Make certain of it, ere it be too late!

Four years later, on the feast day of Wales's patron saint, the preacher himself was taken home. He died of cancer. He lies buried in the cemetery of the Phillips family, from which his wife came, in Newcastle Emlyn, near the farm which had belonged to his mother's people. The words, 'For I determined not to know any thing among you, save Jesus Christ, and him crucified,' are inscribed on his gravestone. Nothing more appropriate could be imagined.

'When nature removes a great man,' said Emerson, 'people explore the horizon for a successor, but none comes and none will. His class is extinguished with him.' That is the case here. There is no-one remotely resembling the Doctor around today, and we are the poorer as a result. To have known him was a supreme privilege, for which I shall always be thankful. His last message to his family, scribbled shakily on a notepad just before he died, when his voice had already gone, was: 'Don't pray for healing; don't try to hold me back from the glory,' and for me those last words, 'the glory', point with precision to the significance that under God he had in my life. He embodied and expressed 'the glory' – the glory of God, of Christ, of grace, of the gospel, of the Christian ministry, of humanness according to the new creation – more richly than any one I have ever known. No-one can give another a greater gift than a vision of such glory as this. I am for ever in his debt.

Amy Carmichael of India

by Elisabeth Elliot

When I was fourteen years old, a student in boarding school, I first heard of Amy Carmichael. The headmistress of the school often quoted her writings and told of her amazing work in India for the rescue of little children in moral danger. No other single individual has had a more powerful influence on my own life and writing than Amy Carmichael. No-one else put the missionary call more clearly.

Of the thirty-six books she wrote, I think it was the little book '*If*' that I read first, and found in it the source of an exhortation we heard often in the evening vespers services: Hold your friends to the highest. '*If*' is a series of statements about love, given to her sentence by sentence, Amy Carmichael claimed, 'almost as if spoken aloud to the inward ear'. Each page holds a single sentence, with the rest of the page blank. Someone has suggested that the blank space is for each of us to write in large letters GUILTY. I was seared by the words.

'If I fear to hold another to the highest because it is so much easier to avoid doing so, then I know nothing of Calvary love.' I was guilty.

'If I can enjoy a joke at the expense of another; if I can in any way slight another in conversation, or even in thought, then I know nothing of Calvary love.' Such jokes, such slights, were habitual with me.

'If I make much of anything appointed, magnify it secretly to myself or insidiously to others . . . then I know nothing of Calvary love.' Every page pointed up my guilt, but every page aroused in me a deep longing to know that love, to be like the one who showed it to us on Calvary, and to follow him.

As a student in college I wrestled with the desperate desire to be married. I had promised the Lord I would go to some foreign land as a missionary, but I hoped I would not be required to go single. By this time I had memorized many of the poems in *Toward Jerusalem*. One of those that became my prayer then, articulating what my heart wanted to say but could not have found the words for was:

> Hold us in quiet through the age-long minute
> While Thou art silent and the wind is shrill:
> Can the boat sink while Thou, dear Lord, art in
> it?
> Can the heart faint that waiteth on Thy will?

There was a strong and practical everyday sort of faith that ran through all her writings, an immediate appropriation of the promises of God and an exquisite artistic sensitivity that drew me like a magnet. I read everything of hers that I could get my hands on, and soon my diaries were peppered with quotations labelled 'AC'.

She was born on 16 December, 1867, in Millisle,

Northern Ireland, of a Scottish Presbyterian flour miller named David Carmichael and his wife Catherine Jane Felson, a doctor's daughter. The eldest of seven children, she often led the rest of them in wild escapades, such as the time she suggested they all eat laburnum pods. She had been told that the pods were poisonous, and thought it would be fun to see how long it would take them to die. They were discovered, and a powerful emetic was administered in time to foil their plans for suicide. Once she led her little brothers up through a skylight on to the slate roof. They slid to the lead gutters and were walking gaily around the edge when they looked down to see their horrified parents staring up at them.

She was educated by governesses before she attended a Wesleyan Methodist boarding school in Harrogate, Yorkshire. It was there she saw that there was something more to do than merely 'nestle' in the love of God, 'something that may be called,' she wrote later, 'coming to Him, or opening the door to Him, or giving oneself to Him. . . . Afterwards, when I began to understand more of what all this meant, I found words which satisfied me. I do not know who wrote them:

'Upon a life I did not live,
Upon a death I did not die,
Another's life, Another's death,
I stake my whole eternity.'

When she was seventeen, seeing on the street in Belfast a poor woman in rags, carrying a heavy bundle, she had what amounted almost to a vision of the things that really matter in life. She and her two brothers, moved with pity for the poor soul, helped her along, though they were embarrassed to be seen with her. Amy described it as a horrid moment, for they were 'not at all exalted Christians', but on they plodded through the grey drizzle.

Suddenly words came to her: 'Gold, silver, precious stones, wood, hay, stubble ... the fire shall try every man's work of what sort it is. If any man's work abide. . . .' From that moment, for the rest of her life, it was eternal things that mattered.

She began children's meetings at home, then moved on to work at the Belfast City Mission, where she taught a boys' class and founded a group for the encouragement of Bible study and prayer called the Morning Watch. On Sunday mornings she taught a class for 'shawlies', working girls who wore shawls because they could not afford hats.

One brother described her as 'a wonderfully sincere, downright, unafraid, and sympathetic sister'. Another said, 'She was determined to get down to the root of things.' Her sister's strongest impression of Amy concerned her enthusiasm. Nothing was impossible.

Her father died when she was eighteen, and the following year brought with it another moment of illumination. At a convention in Glasgow, when her soul seemed to be in a fog, she heard the words of the closing prayer, 'O Lord, we know Thou art able to keep us from falling.' It was as if a light shone for her. When her hostess took her to a restaurant for lunch and the mutton chop was not properly cooked, she remembered years later how trivial the chop was by comparison with those shining words, *able to keep us from falling*.

Her work with the 'shawlies' grew so rapidly that a hall was soon needed that would seat five hundred people. The story of how that hall was paid for by one lady and how the land to put it on was given by the head of the biggest mill in the city is only the beginning of a lifetime of seeing a Heavenly Father's faithful provision for material needs as well as spiritual. She decided against receiving any money from those who were not utterly one with her aims, accepting it only when it was truly given to God. Amy Carmichael prayed for money and it came. She soon saw Bible classes, girls' meetings, mothers' meetings, sewing classes, and gospel meetings being held in the hall, which was called 'The Welcome'.

In 1888 all the family's money was lost, and they moved to England where Amy began another work for factory girls in Manchester.

It was on a snowy evening in January 1892 that a call which she could not escape and dared not resist came clearly: *Go ye*. A long and spiritually harrowing period followed as she sought to weigh her responsibilities to those who had never heard of Christ against responsibilities to her mother and, most agonizingly, to Mr Robert Wilson, one of the founders of the Keswick Convention in England to whom she had become like a beloved daughter. His wife and only daughter had died and Amy had moved into the house. Although the situation was unusual, and not entirely to the liking of Wilson's two bachelor sons who also lived there, she believed it was God's place for her for a time. She loved and revered him, calling him 'the D. O. M.' (Dear Old Man) and 'Fatherie' in letters to her mother. The thought of leaving him was a keen, sharp pain, something she had to lay on the altar, as it were, and trust God to take care of.

She thought of going to Ceylon, but then the knowledge that a million were dying every month without God in China prompted her to offer herself for that land. In July of 1892 she became the first missionary to be supported by the Keswick Convention, and went in September to the China Inland Mission (now OMF) headquarters in London. Geraldine Guinness, who later became the daughter-in-law of the mission's founder, Hudson Taylor, was one of those who encouraged and prayed for her there. She had purchased and packed her outfit when she received word that the doctor refused to pass her for service in China.

It must have been a blow, but did not in the least deter her in her purpose. She knew she had been called, and had no doubt that she would go – somewhere.

She sailed for Japan in 1893 to work under the Reverend Barclay F. Buxton of the Church Missionary Society and plunged into the work with joy, studying the language and adopting Japanese dress almost at once. It was there that she received a letter from her mother, asking whether she loved anybody very much. She gave an evasive answer. This is the only hint to be found anywhere that she might have had a chance to marry and perhaps was forced to choose between a man she loved and the call of God. Of course I am reading a great deal into the few words her biographer uses to cover this question, but because in my own experience it was such a burning one, I often longed to know more. I wished with all my heart that she had not been so everlastingly self-effacing and cautious in keeping herself out of her books.

Within a year, ill health took her to Shanghai, then to Ceylon, and a few months later she returned to England because the D. O. M. had had a stroke. His hopes were raised once more that she would remain with him.

During this time her first book was published, *From Sunrise Land*, a collection of letters she had written in Japan, illustrated with her own sketches. Again she received a medical rejection, and again she faced the unknown, still sure that the Lord who had called her so clearly would open a way somewhere, somehow. At last she was accepted by the Church of England Zenana Missionary Society at Keswick in July 1895 and arrived in Bangalore, India, in December with dengue fever and a temperature of 105. Some missionaries prophesied that she would not last six months. She lasted fifty-five years without a furlough.

Nearly a year later she met a missionary named Walker, who suggested that his district, Tinnevelly, was a much better place than Bangalore to learn Tamil, the language which the mission had assigned her to learn. Walker offered to be her teacher, and so it was in December 1896 that she reached the place which would be home for the rest of her life.

She was an excellent student. It was not that the language came easily to her. She prayed and trusted God for help, but she did what God could not do for her – she studied. She took comfort from the words of Numbers 22:28, 'The Lord opened the mouth of the ass.'

Amy lived with the Walkers in two different towns, where the number of Christians was pitifully small. She gathered together a band of Indian women to itinerate with her, among whom was Ponnammal, who was to become an intimate, lifelong friend. They travelled at the rate of two or three miles an hour in a bullock bandy, a two-wheeled springless cart with a mat roof, 'bang over stones and slabs of rock, down on one side, up on the other. Once we went smoothly down a bank and into a shallow swollen pool, and the water swished in at the lower end and floated our books out quietly' (*Things as They Are*, p. 5). They camped near the village at night, visiting in homes or wherever they could find women or children to talk to. Sometimes Walker and some of the men joined them for open-air meetings in the evening.

It was no lark. They found themselves in battle – the Lord's battle, to be sure, but one in which they were his warriors, up against a stupendous force comprising principalities, powers, rulers of darkness, potentialities unknown and unimagined. She tried to describe it in a book called *Things as They Are*, but 'How can we describe it?' she wrote. 'What we have seen and tried to describe is only an indication of Something undescribed, and is as nothing in comparison with it.' Nevertheless, even the understatement that she did put down on paper was rejected by publishers. It was much too discouraging.

People wanted pleasanter stories, happier endings, so the manuscript was put in a drawer for several years until some English friends visited her, saw with their own eyes the truth of things, and begged her to allow them to try again to find a publisher willing to risk it. The book appeared in 1903. Its accuracy was questioned, so when a fourth edition was called for, letters were included from missionaries in India confirming in the strongest terms what she had written.

Amy had a clear eye and a keen ear. She wrote what she saw and heard, not what missionary magazines might have conditioned her to see and hear. One of them, for example, stated that Indian women think English women 'fairer and more divine than anything imagined'. But Amy heard them say when they saw her, 'What an appalling spectacle! A great white man!' 'Why no jewels? What relations? Where are they all? Why have you left them and come here? What does the government give you for coming here?'

'An old lady with fluffy white hair leaned forward and gazed at me with a beautiful, earnest gaze. She did not speak; she just listened and gazed, "drinking it all in". And then she raised a skeleton claw, grabbed her hair and pointed to mine. "Are you a widow too", she asked, "that you have no oil on yours?" After a few such experiences that beautiful gaze loses its charm.'

The notion of hungry 'souls' eagerly thronging to hear the gospel story is an appealing one and perhaps represents a true picture in some places, but certainly not in South India, or, I found, in South America. I was very thankful for that book. *Things as They Are* told it to me straight, and thus prepared me for my own missionary work as few other books besides the Bible had done. It told of the great fortresses which are Hindu temples, and of the wickedness practised there. It told of the utter indifference of most of the people when told of the love of

Jesus. It told, too, of the few who wanted to hear.

'Tell me, what is the good of your Way? Will it fill the cavity within me?' one old woman asked, striking herself a resounding smack on the stomach. 'Will it stock my paddy-pots or nourish my bulls or cause my palms to bear good juice? If it will not do all these good things, what is the use of it?'

It told of a boy who confessed Christ, an only son, heir to considerable property. He was tied up and flogged but he never wavered. At last he had to choose between his home and Christ. He chose Christ. The whole clan descended on the missionaries' bungalow, sat on the floor in a circle and pleaded. 'A single pulse seemed to beat in the room, so tense was the tension, until he spoke out bravely. "I will not go back", he said.' Though they promised him everything – houses, lands, a rich wife with many jewels – if only he would not break caste, though they told him how his mother neither ate not slept but sat with hair undone, wailing the death-wail for her son, he would not go back. Later, Shining of Life (for that was his name) was baptized, and within a few weeks was dead of cholera. As he lay dying they taunted him. 'This is your reward for breaking your caste!' 'Do not trouble me,' he answered, pointing upward. 'This is the way by which I am going to Jesus.'

During those first years, Amy Carmichael learned of the hideous traffic in little girls for temple prostitution. Calling them 'the most defenceless of God's innocent little creatures', she gave herself to save them. She prayed for a way – she had not the least idea how it could be done, but she knew her master, knew his limitless power and believed him to show her.

She wrote letters (veiled, always, because the things she saw and heard were unprintable then) asking for prayer. She asked God to give her the words to say which would arouse Christians.

And thus God answered me: 'Thou shalt have
  words,
But at this cost, that thou must first be burnt,
Burnt by red embers from a secret fire,
Scorched by fierce heats and withering winds
  that sweep
Through all thy being, carrying thee afar
From old delights. . . .'

In 1900 Amy went with the Walkers to camp in a quiet, out-of-the-way village called Dohnavur, and a year later the first temple child was brought to Amy, a girl of seven named Preena, whose hands had been branded with hot irons when she had once attempted to escape. Gradually the child had learned that she was to be 'married to the god'. She knew enough to detest the prospect and fled to a Christian woman who took her to Amy Carmichael. 'When she saw me,' Preena wrote fifty years later, 'the first thing she did was to put me on her lap and kiss me. I thought, "my mother used to put me on her lap and kiss me – who is the person who kisses me like my mother?" From that day she became my mother, body and soul.'

And from that time on Amy Carmichael was called *Amma* (accent on the last syllable), the Tamil word for mother.

She began to uncover the facts of temple life. It was a system that had obtained from the ninth or tenth century. The girls trained for this service were sometimes given by their families, sometimes sold, usually between the ages of five and eight, but often when they were babies. They were certainly not 'unwanted' children. They were very much wanted. In order to insure that they did not try to run away, they were shut up in back rooms, carefully watched, and, if they tried to escape, tortured as Preena was. They were trained in music and dancing, and, of course, introduced to the mysteries of the oldest profession in the world.

Amma's search for the children covered three years, but at last, one by one, they began to be brought to her. Soon it became necessary for her to have a settled place. Dohnavur, which she had thought of only as a campsite, proved to be the perfect answer. Indian women joined her, willing to do the humble, humdrum, relentless work of caring for children, work that they saw as truly spiritual work because it was done first of all for the love of Christ.

By 1906 there were fifteen babies, three nurses and five convent girls training as nurses. There were no doctors or nurses to begin with, of course, not even any wet-nurses to help with the babies, since it was not the custom for village women to breast-feed a child other than their own. A number of babies died, some because they were frail when they arrived, some due to epidemics, some for lack of human milk. Amma grieved as any mother grieves, for they were her very own children. When one of the loveliest of them, a baby girl named Indraneela, died, Amma wrote:

> Dear little hands, outstretched in eager
> welcome,
> Dear little head, that close against me lay –
> Father, to Thee I give my Indraneela,
> Thou wilt take care of her until That Day.

In 1907 came the first gift of money to build a nursery. It was not long before Amma learned that boys, too, were being used for immoral purposes in the dramatic societies. Prayer began to go up for them, and by 1918 the work expanded to include them.

There were no salaried workers, either Indian or foreign, in the Dohnavur Fellowship. All gave themselves for love of the Lord, and no appeal was ever made for funds. When one sentence in a book she had written might have been construed as an appeal, Amma withdrew the book from circulation. No-one was ever authorized to make pleas for money on their behalf. Needs were mentioned only to God, and God supplied them. The work grew until by 1950 or thereabouts the 'Family' numbered over nine hundred people, including children and Indian and European workers. There was a hospital, many nurseries and bungalows for the children and their *accals* (sisters, as the Indian workers were called), a House of Prayer, classrooms, workrooms, storehouses, hostels, playing fields, fruit and vegetable gardens, farm and pasture lands. It was all 'given'. The financial policy has not changed to this day. The Unseen Leader is still in charge, and from him comes all that is needed from day to day, from hammocks in which the tiniest newborns swing, to modern equipment for the hospital. There are doctors, nurses, teachers, builders, engineers, farmers, craftsmen, cooks. There are none who are *only* preachers. A Hindu had once said to someone in the Dohnavur Fellowship, 'We have heard the preaching, but *can you show us the life of your Lord Jesus*?' Each worker, whatever his practical task, seeks to show that life as he offers his service to his Lord.

The books *Nor Scrip, Tables in the Wilderness, Meal in a Barrel*, and *Windows* are records of God's constant provision for material needs, story after amazing story of his timing, his resources, his chosen instruments. The God who could provide food for a prophet through the instrumentality of ravens and a poor widow, was trusted to meet the daily needs of children and those who cared for them, a few rupees here, a few thousand pounds there.

In 1943 she wrote:

> An immense amount of rice is required for a family of nearly eight hundred, not counting

> guests and the poorest of the ill in the Place of Healing. Rice is brought from the fields unhusked. There has to be room for parboiling, drying, husking and storing. Quantities of other things have to be stored; palmyra-palm sugar, coconuts, tamarind pods, vegetables and fruit from our gardens, besides the spices which make curry what it is. And there are tins of oil, sacks of salt, shelves of soap. Then there are the miscellanea usually called sundries, such as lanterns, lamp-oil, rope, mats, extra cooking vessels, brass vessels, stocks of pots and pans, buckets and so on.
>
> *Though the Mountains Shake*, p. 233.

'And He said to them, "When I sent you out with no purse or bag or sandals, did you lack anything?" They said, "Nothing"' (Lk. 22:35).

Amma was a woman of great reserve. Loving, unselfish and outgoing to others, she was acutely aware of the dangers of drawing attention to herself in any way, or of drawing people to herself rather than to Christ. She could easily have become a cult figure, having great gifts of personality, leadership and the ability to encourage the gifts of others. But she held strictly to Christ as leader and Lord, and 'coveted no place on earth but the dust at the foot of the Cross'. In January 1919, her name appeared on the Royal Birthday Honours List. She wrote to Lord Pentland, 'Would it be unpardonably rude to ask to be allowed not to have it? . . . I have done nothing to make it fitting, and cannot understand it at all. It troubles me to have an experience so different from His Who was despised and rejected – not kindly honoured.' She was persuaded at last that she could not refuse it, but she did not go to Madras for the presentation ceremony.

There are a few pictures of her in the biography, but too

few. I would love to have seen many more, but she refused to allow them to be taken, and although there are many pictures of the children and Indian workers in the books she wrote, none are included of herself or of other European workers.

Her biographer, Bishop Frank Houghton, tells us only that she was of medium height with brown eyes and brown hair. When I asked a member of the Fellowship to describe her she smiled. All she could think to say was, 'She had wonderful eyes.'

The light that seemed to shine in and through and around this woman was love. When asked what they remembered best about her, many people answered *love*. There is hardly a page of her books that does not speak of it in some way. Her poems are full of it.

> Love through me, Love of God . . .
> O love that faileth not, break forth,
> And flood this world of Thine.
> (*Toward Jerusalem*, p. 11)

> Pour through me now: I yield myself to Thee,
> Love, blessed Love, do as Thou wilt with me.
> (p. 69)

> O the Passion of Thy Loving,
> O the Flame of Thy desire!
> Melt my heart with Thy great loving,
> Set me all aglow, afire. (p. 83)

When she thought her time on earth was nearly up she began to write letters to each one of the Family, which she put into a box to be opened after her death. These letters are steeped in love. One of them speaks of a misunderstanding that had arisen between two members of the Fellowship, and how deeply it had hurt her to hear of it.

'Refuse it. Hate it,' she wrote. 'It may seem a trifle, but it is of hell. . . . If this were the last time I could speak to you I should say just these words, "Beloved, let us love!" My children, our comrades in the War of the Lord, I say these words to you again, "Beloved, let us love!" . . . We perish if we do not love.'

The kind of love she lived and taught was no mere matter of feelings. It was steel. Though for many years she made it a practice to give each child a good-night kiss, she also believed in canings when canings were called for, but then she would wipe away the tears with her handkerchief. Sometimes she would pray with the child first, that the punishment might help her, and, after she had administered it, she found on at least one occasion that a glass of water effectively silenced the howls.

In her book about the spiritual training of an Indian nurse named Kohila she writes:

> It was when she was given charge of a nursery with younger girls to train and to influence that the first difficulty appeared. . . . The alloy that was discovered in her gold was a weakness which leaned towards shielding a wrongdoer, or even sympathising with her, rather than taking the harder way of love without dissimulation, the noblest kind of help that soul can offer soul, and by far the most costly.
>
> Once, and this was indeed a grevious time, a special friend of Kohila's caused a younger one to stumble by teaching her to deceive. Kohila's judgment was influenced by her fondness for her friend. She admitted the wrongdoing but condoned it. . . . She forgot her Lord's solemn words about the millstone and the sea. Her sympathy was rather with the offender than with Him who was offended in the offence done to His little one.

> But syrupy affection never yet led to spiritual integrity. And though it looks so like the charity which is greater than faith and hope that it is 'admired of many', it is not admirable. It is sin. And it is blinding sin (*Kohila*, p. 75).

Again, in the little book '*If*':

> If I am afraid to speak the truth, lest I lose affection, or lest the one concerned should say, 'You do not understand' or because I fear to lose my reputation for kindness; if I put my own good name before the other's highest good, then I know nothing of Calvary love. (p. 24)

One day in 1916 when the World War shadowed them with fear for the future, a group of seven Indian girls met with Amma to join themselves together as 'The Sisters of the Common Life'. They were young women who wanted to live a life of unreserved devotion, 'a life without fences'. They took their name from the Brotherhood of the Common Life, a religious community founded in about 1380 in Holland by Gerhard Groot. They determined that there would be no line drawn between the spiritual and the secular, for Jesus drew no such line. Amma believed that the usual teaching about Mary and Martha was all wrong. It was not service that the Lord rebuked, but fuss. 'The spirit can sit at the Master's feet while the hands are at work for others. Come unto Me and rest – take My yoke upon you.'

If a job was to be done that nobody else wanted to do, someone would say, 'Ask her. She is a Sister of the Common Life.' They were ready to go to any lengths and to lay down their lives for others. They read books together in English, for the spiritual classics that had put iron into Amma's soul were not translated into Tamil.

They were single women who believed it was God's will for them to remain single in order to serve him without distraction. Theirs was meant to be a life of joy, with nothing 'dreary and doubtful' about it. It was a soldier's life. 'The nearer the soldier is to the Captain the more he will be attacked by the enemy' (*Amy Carmichael of Dohnavur*, p. 219).

There were no vows in the technical sense. If any of them felt that God was giving them marriage, they could leave with no stigma attached to their leaving, but as long as they were in the group they acknowledged the cross as the attraction. These were their rules:

> *My Vow:* Whatsoever Thou sayest unto me, by Thy grace I will do it.
> *My Constraint:* Thy love, O Christ my Lord.
> *My Confidence:* Thou art able to keep that which I have committed unto Thee.
> *My Joy:* To do Thy will, O God.
> *My Discipline:* That which I would not choose, but which Thy love appoints.
> *My Prayer:* Conform my will to Thine.
> *My Motto:* Love to live: Live to love.
> *My Portion:* The Lord is the portion of mine inheritance.
>
> Teach us, good Lord, to serve Thee more faithfully; to give and not to count the cost; to fight and not to heed the wounds; to toil and not to seek for rest; to labour and not to ask for any reward, save that of knowing that we do Thy will, O Lord our God.

Amy Carmichael has been accused of opposing marriage as though it were God's 'second best'. It is a false accusation. She understood the power of the influence of a Christian home, and many of the children from

Dohnavur as well as many of the workers have married. Some of these have continued as a part of the Dohnavur Fellowship. But she believed exactly what Paul believed, that those who do marry will have 'trouble in the flesh', and cannot possibly be as free as the unmarried for certain tasks in the Lord's service. Many single women were needed to mother the hundreds of children. As boys were included, men were needed also, but the number of men who regarded celibacy as a divine call was small.

Amma was a woman peculiarly sensitive to beauty, as not only her writings but everything she touched will show. She was determined, as plans for each building were drawn up, that they should be beautiful. When they were planning the hospital, Dr Murray Webb-Peploe asked if it might be too expensive. She hesitated to answer, but the next day was 4 June, for which the verse in the *Daily Light*, that marvellous little book of collected scriptures, was, 'The house that is to be builded for the Lord must be exceeding magnifical.' She took the word magnifical to mean 'perfect for its purpose of glorifying the God of love, so that men and women will be drawn to Him. He is also the God of beauty, and it follows that ugliness jars. He has no pleasure in it – nor in dirt.'

The long poems, *Pool* and *The Valley of Vision*, contain exquisite descriptions of the loveliness of the world around her, but delve deep into the mystery of its sorrow and suffering,

> I saw a scarf of rainbow water-lace,
> Blue-green, green-blue, lilac and violet.
> Light, water, air, it trailed, a phantom thing,
> An iridescence, vanishing as I gazed;
> Like wings of dragonflies, a hint and gone –
> Discovery was very near me then.
> But no unseemly, no irreverent haste
> Perplexes him who stands alone with God

In upland places. Presently I saw . . .
Father, who speakest to us by the way,
Now from a burning bush, now by a stream. . . .

Hers was a mystical mind. A true mystic is an utterly pratical person, for he sees the Real as no pedant can ever see it, he finds the spiritual in the material (what T. S. Eliot calls 'fear in a handful of dust', or Thomas Howard, 'splendour in the ordinary'). George MacDonald said: 'A mystical mind is one which, having perceived that the highest expression of which truth admits, lies in the symbolism of nature and the human customs that result from human necessities, prosecutes thought about truth so embodied by dealing with the symbols themselves after logical forms' (*Unspoken Sermons*).

She was logical. She was incisive, vigorous, utterly clear. She could write of a 'scarf of rainbow water-lace' or she could use words that stab like a dagger or scorch like fire: 'And we talked of the difference between the fleshly love and the spiritual; the two loves stood out in sharp distinction. In such an hour the fire of the love of God is searching. It knows just where to find the clay in us. That clay must be turned to crystal' (*Ploughed Under*, p. 187).

To modern ears it seems marvellous that a woman with what would seem to us little formal education and with no 'degrees' should be able to use the English language so flawlessly, to shape a phrase so finely, and to write (very rapidly – sometimes twelve to fifteen hours a day) with such apparent ease and fluidity. There is not a word in any book or poem which Amy Carmichael had not bought by suffering. There is not an empty word, a superfluous word, a glib word. Every word, every line, has work to do.

In my recent rereading of the biography I found illumination of many passages which echo in my memory from her own writings. I found the circumstances which gave rise to those writings, the context in which she learned the lessons so lucidly set forth. Words given to her in the heat of battle have spoken strongly to me in the heat of my own experiences. They have been, in fact, the very voice of God to me, alive and powerful and sharp today as they were thirty or twenty-five or ten years ago.

There are markings, of course, in my copies of Amy Carmichael's books, as there are markings in every book on my shelves in which I have found real meat. The Amy Carmichael books in their uniform blue covers with lotus motif take up only half a shelf now, which makes me sad. Some of them have been 'borrowed' and never found their way home. Others, to my great consternation, I left in a jungle house in Ecuador. Those I have are well-worn. Most bear the marks of mould and mildew and crickets, but they are my trusted friends. When I was in the throes of decision as to whether, newly widowed, I should take my small daughter and go to live with a remote tribe of Indians, I circled these words:

> His thoughts said, How can I know that it is the time to move?
>
> His Father said, And it shall be when thou shalt hear a sound of going in the tops of mulberry trees, that then thou shalt go out to battle. Thou shalt certainly hear that sound. [That sentence is underlined.] There will be a quiet sense of sureness and a sense of peace.
>
> (*His Thoughts Said . . . His Father Said*, 16)

I remember feeling doubtful about that 'sound of going' in mulberry trees. There were no such trees in our jungle. Of course I knew that the words came from Scripture (2 Sa. 5:24 AV), but Amma had a disconcerting habit of quoting from many diverse sources, including the Bible, without citing the reference, and often without using quotation marks. It is flattering to the reader that she supposed us to be as well-read as she, and as spiritually advanced. I wasn't and I'm not, but I can testify to the truth of what she wrote. The 'sound of going' was different for her at different times, I'm sure, and the sign given to me in 1958 which led to my going to those Indians was not in any mulberry trees. But I found the promise fulfilled. 'Thou shalt certainly hear that sound.' God made it perfectly plain when the time came. I understood then her confidence, the sense of sureness and peace.

But subsequent decisions have put me in the same sort of quandary, and I have gone back again to the same little book.

> But the son still wondered what he should do if he did not hear a Voice directing him, till he came to understand that, as he waited, his Father would work and would so shape the events of common life that they would become indications of His will. He has shown also that they would be in accord with some word of Scripture which would be laid upon his heart.
>
> (19)

That made sense to me. No audible voices have ever told me what to do, but the providential shaping of events and corroborating scriptures given to me at the time have proved again and again the trustworthiness of the shepherd.

There have been one or two occasions when I have been falsely accused by people on whom I had once had an influence for good. It is a hard lesson to learn, and I am a slow disciple. There is a circle around this one:

> Was He, whom he called Master and Lord, always understood? Was He never misjudged?

> They laid to His charge things that He knew not, to the great discomfiture of His spirit. Is it not enough for the disciple that he be as his Master and the servant as his Lord? (57)

Amma was visiting one day in 1931 in a nearby village where there had been hostility to Christians. She fell into a pit which had been dug 'where no pit should be'. The injuries did not heal, and she suffered acute neuritis in her right arm, arthritis in her back, chronic infections, and the cumulative effects of stress for the rest of her life, hardly leaving her room until she died in January 1951 at the age of eighty-three. During those twenty years as an invalid, in nearly constant pain, she wrote fifteen books 'out of the furnace', as it were, and the words of 2 Corinthians 1 show a part of the service God gave her to do:

> Praise be to the God and Father of our Lord Jesus Christ, the all-merciful Father, the God whose consolation never fails us! He comforts us in all our troubles, so that we in turn may be able to comfort others in any trouble of theirs and to share with them the consolation we ourselves receive from God. As Christ's cup of suffering overflows, and we suffer with him, so also through Christ our consolation overflows. If distress be our lot, it is the price we pay for your consolation, for your salvation (2 Cor. 1:3–6).

I am one of the many thousands, surely, for whose consolation and salvation Amy Carmichael paid a heavy price. That she paid it with gladness and a whole heart no-one who has read even a page of hers could possibly doubt.

As I write these pages, my husband hands me a newspaper telling of the life of Henry Morrison Flagler, the American millionaire responsible for developing Palm Beach, Florida, as a playground for the very rich. In the early 1890s, the account states, he was looking for his life's 'crowning challenge'. It was, I remembered, a snowy night in 1892 when Amy Carmichael heard the call she could not escape and dared not resist: *Go ye*.

In 1894 Flagler built the Royal Poinciana, the world's largest resort hotel, accommodating two thousand. In that year Amy Carmichael was in Japan, where she wrote:

> O for a passionate passion for souls,
> O for a pity that yearns!
> O for the love that loves unto death,
> O for the fire that burns!

In 1896 Flagler opened his Palm Beach Inn, later to become The Breakers. That was the year in which Amma reached Tinnevelly, the part of South India where she would live out the rest of her life of service.

In 1901 Flagler's luxurious Whitehall, a marble palace built for his third wife, had been completed at the cost of four million dollars. In 1901 Preena, the first temple child, came to Amma, which meant the beginning of what would become the Dohnavur Fellowship.

'The Vanderbilts, Wanamakers, Astors, Goulds, Belmonts, and European royalty come to the magic island,' the newspaper goes on, 'awash in Caribbean splendour and Henry Morrison Flagler's grandeur.'

'Gold, silver, precious stones, wood, hay, stubble . . . the fire shall try every man's work of what sort it is.' These were the words that had come to Amy as a girl, when she stumbled along that Belfast street with the ragged old woman, words that defined for her for ever the nature of man's choices. 'If any man's work abide . . . he shall receive a reward' (1 Cor. 3:14).

Like the mountaineer whose epitaph she loved to

quote, she 'died climbing'. Now she is one of the great cloud of witnesses whose course has been finished, and who cheer us on to run the race that is set before us, looking as they did to Jesus, 'who for the joy that was set before him, endured the cross.'

Sources

For information about the life of Amy Carmichael, I have relied on Frank Houghton's *Amy Carmichael of Dohnavur* (SPCK, 1953) and on the following books by Amy Carmichael:

His Thoughts Said . . . His Father Said(SPCK, 1941).
'If' (SPCK, 1938).
Kohila (SPCK, 1939).
Ploughed Under (SPCK, 1934).
Things as They Are (Morgan and Scott, 1903).
Though the Mountains Shake (Loizeaux Bros., New York, 1946).
Toward Jerusalem (SPCK, 1936).

William Wilberforce

by Charles Colson

SEVERAL HUNDRED MILES OFF THE COAST OF AFRICA, 1787. The scudding clouds obscured the moon as the heavy schooner pitched forward in the dark waters. The decks were empty save for the lone sailor on the late watch and a cluster of others at the wheel.

The rest of the crew tossed fitfully in their hammocks; in the main cabin a fat tallow candle burned low, flickering in the tropical air. The captain, a balding man with thick sideburns, squinted as he dipped his quill in a well of sepia ink and continued his log report, laboriously noting progress on their voyage to Jamaica. The flogging that day of the cabin boy was the only incident of note.

In the dark hold below, the heavy air was almost palpable with the stench of human waste and vomit. Five hundred and twelve black men and women lay on their sides in the filth, crammed so tightly together that the chest of each was pressed against the sweaty back of his or her neighbour, their legs drawn up, their feet on the heads of those in the next anguished row.

Moans, sobs, and feverish delirium combined with the creaks of the ship's aged timbers to transform the putrid hold into a scene from hell.

And for the slaves, it was. They were captured Africans, some the prisoners of tribal wars or petty criminals, others the unsuspecting dinner guests of visiting Englishmen. But all had been rounded up, chained and held in a stockade, then sold to the highest bidder who had come into port.

The elderly and unfit had been dispatched with a pistol shot or clubbed to death, their bodies dragged into the shallows, where they bobbed gently until caught in the flow of the tide.

Others were branded, then whipped and shoved into small boats to be ferried to the large ocean-going vessels lying at anchor offshore. Weeping, screaming for mercy, they were hoisted on to the tall ship and forced into the stinking hold, then shackled into irons.

But not all were immediately driven below. The crew, though diseased and ill-treated themselves, claimed the one sordid privilege of their trade – the pick of the slave women. Once off the coast, the ship became half bedlam, half brothel, as one captain put it.

Now on this cloudy night, several weeks into the voyage, sixty slaves were already dead. Some had succumbed to the fevers raging through the rotten hold. Others, driven insane by the horrors, were disposed of by the crew. Each morning as the lower decks were opened, the dead and the near-dead were removed, their bodies thrown overboard to the waiting sharks.

Whenever the captain watched this morning ritual, he cursed as each black body hit the choppy water, muttering as he calculated his lost profits. Certainly, however, he had no legal worries about throwing sick slaves to their deaths: in a celebrated case in England's high court only four years earlier, slaves had been described as 'goods and chattels', the Chief Justice observing that it was 'exactly as if horses had been thrown overboard'. And in the colonies, the word of a black could not be taken over a white. That was the law.

At any rate, none of the slaves remaining in the dark hold of that slave ship had any idea what was in store if they did survive the three-month journey: they would be auctioned naked in the marketplace, then – if they survived the treatment of their new masters – life would be merely a dogged hold on survival in the cane fields. A slave would never know or see in his or her short lifespan the nation which would so richly profit from their misery, England.

LONDON, 1787. In the city described as 'one vast casino', the rich counted their profits from the slave trade while in a fog of claret. They lost and rewon their fortunes over gaming tables in prestigious private clubs; duels were the order of the day to preserve honour.

Corruption in government was so widespread that very few Members of Parliament thought twice about the common practice of buying votes. And since the slave trade was not only considered successful business, but a national policy, political alliances revolved around commitment to the trade. It become euphemistically known as 'the institution', the 'pillar and support of British plantation industry in the West Indies'.

The planters and gentlemen who grew rich through the profits of their trade investments became an increasingly powerful force in Parliament, paying £3,000 to £5,000 to 'buy' boroughs, which sent their representatives to the House of Commons; hence the term 'rotten boroughs'. Their influence grew until a large bloc of the House was controlled by the vested influence of the slave traders.

The same attitude reigned in the House of Lords. After all, the horrors of the trade were far away and unseen. But the returns on their investment were often 100 per cent; the cotton and sugar and profits the slaves provided were very tangible. If the slave trade made England stronger – and the rich richer – it could not be a bad thing.

So they counted their returns and, when time weighed heavy on their hands, turned to whatever distraction took their fancy. The town's theatres were surrounded by clusters of brothels; hordes of prostitutes (estimated at one out of every four women in the city) specialized in any manner of perversion for those whose appetites had grown jaded.

High society similarly revolved around romantic intrigue and adulterous affairs. An upper-class couple might not see one another in public for weeks during the social season; no self-respecting hostess would have such poor taste as to invite a husband and wife to the same social event.

The poor had no such opportunity to escape from one another. Crammed together in grimy cobble-stoned streets, they sweated out a living as cogs in Britain's emerging industrial machine. Pale children worked as many as eighteen hours a day in the cotton mills or coal mines, bringing home a few shillings a month to their parents, who often spent it on cheap gin. One-eighth of the deaths in London were attributed to excessive drinking.

Highwaymen were folk heroes. Newgate and other infamous prisons overflowed with debtors, murderers, children and rapists. A twelve-year-old thief might be hung the same day as a celebrated robber, with huge crowds relishing the expiration of the celebrity while scarcely noticing the life choking out of the other.

Frequently executions provided one form of public

amusement, bull baiting another. Bulls were tortured with fire or acid to keep them lively and if the attacking dogs failed to be gored, their throats would be slashed to satisfy the crowd's thirst for blood. At county fairs, badgers, their tails nailed to the ground, were worried to death by dogs; sheep were slaughtered as savagely as possible for popular sport.

At one such event, the Duke of Bedford and a Lord Barrymore staged a bet in which the latter, for £500, brought forth a man who ate a live cat before a cheering crowd.

In short, London was the centre of a country where unchecked human passions had run their course. Few were the voices raised in opposition.

4 OLD PALACE YARD, LONDON, 25 OCTOBER, 1787. It was still dark when the slight young man pulled the dressing gown around his small, thin frame and sat at the oak desk in the second floor library. As he adjusted the flame of his lamp, the warm light shone on his piercing blue eyes, oversized nose and high wrinkling forehead – an agile face that reflected the turmoil of his thoughts as he eyed the jumble of pamphlets on the cluttered desk. They were all on the same subject – the horrors of the slave trade.

He ran his hand through his wavy hair and opened his well-worn Bible. He would begin this day, as was his custom, with a time of personal prayer and Scripture reading. But his thoughts kept returning to the pamphlets' grisly accounts of human flesh being sold, like so much cattle, for the profit of his countrymen. He couldn't wipe the scenes from his mind. Something inside him – that insistent conviction he'd felt before – was telling him that all that had happened in his life had been for a purpose, preparing him to meet that barbaric evil head-on.

William Wilberforce was born in Hull in 1759, the only son of a prosperous merchant family. Though an average student at Cambridge, his quick wit made him a favourite among his fellows, including William Pitt, who shared his interest in politics. Often the two young men spent their evenings in the gallery of the House of Commons, watching the heated debates over the American war.

After graduation, Wilberforce stood as Conservative parliamentary candidate for his home town of Hull. He was only twenty-one – but the prominence of his family, his speaking ability, and a generous feast he sponsored for voters on election day carried the contest.

When he arrived in London, the city's elegant private clubs and societies welcomed him. Wilberforce soon fell in step, happily concentrating on the pursuit of pleasure and political advancement.

He spent his evenings with friends, consuming enormous dinners accompanied by multiple bottles of wine and then perhaps a play, dancing, or a night of gambling. His friendship with William Pitt and other young politicians flourished. Then, in early 1784, Pitt, though only twenty-four, was elected prime minister. Inspired, Wilberforce took a big political gamble, standing for election for both his safe seat in Hull and as one of two MPs for the county of Yorkshire, the largest and most influential constituency in the country.

It was a gruelling campaign, the outcome uncertain until the closing day, when Wilberforce addressed a large rally. James Boswell, Samuel Johnson's celebrated biographer, stood in the cold rain and watched Wilberforce, barely over five feet tall, prepare to address the wet, bored crowd. 'I saw what seemed a mere shrimp mount upon the table,' Boswell wrote later, 'but as I listened, he grew and grew, until the shrimp became a whale.'

Such was the power of the young parliamentarian's oratory that he was elected as member for both Hull and Yorkshire simultaneously. As an intimate of the prime minister, respected by both political parties, William Wilberforce seemed destined for power and prominence.

After the election, Wilberforce's mother invited him to join his sister and several cousins on a tour of the Continent. Wilberforce agreed, then ran into his old schoolmaster from Hull, Isaac Milner, and spontaneously asked him to join the travelling party.

That holiday was to change Wilberforce's life.

Isaac Milner was a stocky, big-boned man with a mind as robust as his body. He was eager to debate with the quick young orator, though he could not match his skill. As their carriage ran over the rutted roads between Nice and the Swiss Alps, their lively discussion turned to religion. Wilberforce, who considered his flirtation with the Methodists – as the religious enthusiasts of his day were known – a childish excess, treated the subject flippantly. Milner growled at his derisive wit, stared moodily out the carriage window, and declared, 'I am no match for you . . . but if you really want to discuss these subjects seriously, I will gladly enter on them with you.'

Provoked by the older man's remark, Wilberforce entered in, eventually agreeing to read the Scriptures daily.

As the summer session of Parliament got underway, Wilberforce returned to the whirl of the London social scene. But his diary reveals subtle changes in his tastes. One party, of the kind he routinely attended, was now described as 'indecent'; his letters began to show concern for corruptions he had scarcely noticed before. The seeds of change had been planted.

During the autumn of 1785, as he and Milner returned to the Continent to continue their tour, Wilberforce was no longer frivolous. He pressed his companion about the Scriptures. The rest of the party complained about their preoccupation as they studied a Greek New Testament in their coach between cities.

Wilberforce returned to London in early November 1785 faced with a decision he could no longer avoid. He knew the choice before him: on one hand his own ambition, his friends, his achievements; on the other a clear call from Jesus Christ.

Selections from his diary show the Holy Spirit's relentless pursuit:

> *27 Nov.*: I must awake to my dangerous state, and never be at rest till I have made my peace with God. My heart is so hard, my blindness so great, that I cannot get a due hatred of sin, though I see I am all corrupt, and blinded to the perception of spiritual things.
>
> *28 Nov.*: Lord, I am wretched, and miserable, and blind, and naked. What infinite love, that Christ should die to save such a sinner, and how necessary is it He should save us altogether, that we may appear before God with nothing of our own!
>
> *29 Nov.*: Pride is my greatest stumbling block...
>
> *30 Nov.*: Was very fervent in prayer this morning, and thought these warm impressions would never go off. Yet in vain endeavour in the evening to rouse myself.... What can so strongly show the stony heart? O God, give me a heart of flesh!...

On 2 December, weary and in need of counsel, Wilberforce resolved to seek out a spiritual guide. He made a fascinating but unlikely choice: John Newton.

The son of a sailor, Newton had gone to sea at the age of eleven, where he eventually deserted, was flogged, and exchanged to a slave ship. Later, Newton himself became a slave on an island off the coast of Africa. Rescued by his father, he sailed on a slave ship and in 1750 was given command of his own slaver. Then, on a passage to the West Indies, Newton was converted to Jesus Christ, later expressing his wonder at the gift of salvation to 'a wretch like me' in his famous hymn, *Amazing Grace.*

Newton was subsequently ordained in the Church of England. His outspoken singlemindedness in spiritual matters must have attracted a buffeted Wilberforce.

Though he cautioned Newton in a note to 'remember that I must be in secret . . . the face of a Member of Parliament is pretty well known', he called on the old preacher. Newton reassured him and, prophetically, told Wilberforce to follow Christ but not to abandon public office: 'The Lord has raised you up to the good of his church and for the good of the nation.'

Wilberforce knew he had to share his new faith with his old friends. The responses were predictable: some thought his mind had snapped under the pressures of work; many were convinced his new-found belief would require him to retreat from public life. Still others were simply bewildered: how could a well-bred and educated young man, with so much promise, get caught up in the religious exuberance of Methodism, a sect appealing only to the common masses?

The reaction Wilberforce cared about most was Pitt's. He wrote to the prime minister, telling him that though he would remain his faithful friend, he could 'no more be so much of a party man as before'.

Pitt's understanding reply revealed the depth of their friendship. But after their first face-to-face discussion,

Wilberforce wrote in his diary: 'He tried to reason me out of my convictions but soon found himself unable to combat their correctness, if Christianity was true. The fact is, he was so absorbed in politics, that he had never given himself time for due reflection on religion.'

Though Pitt and Wilberforce were to continue as friends and allies, their relationship would never again be the same. And, indeed, one of the great sorrows of Wilberforce's life was that the friend he cared for most never accepted the God he loved more.

On this foggy Sunday morning in 1787, as Wilberforce sat at his desk, he reflected that even if Pitt did not share his commitment to Christ, God had brought him brothers who did. He thought about Thomas Clarkson, the red-headed clergyman and brilliant essayist who had visited so often that year while Wilberforce had been ill – Clarkson, whose passion for justice and righteousness awed him.

These were Clarkson's pamphlets strewn across his desk, shocking papers detailing the brutality of the slave trade. Wilberforce had been poring over them for months. He stared out of the window at the grey English drizzle, but all he could see were burdened slave ships leaving the sun-baked coasts of Africa.

Then, on the cobble-stoned street below, two cloaked figures stumbled into view, leaning heavily on one another. Their raucous voices jangled together in a few bars of a lewd song as they lurched towards home, near collapse after a long night of carousing. Such a common sight in London.

He turned back to the desk and the journal filled with tiny, cramped writing meant for no-one's eyes but his own. He thought about his conversion – had God saved him only for the eternal rescue of his own soul, or also to bring his light to the world around him? He could not be content with the comfort of life at Palace Yard, the stimulating debates in Parliament. . . . True Christianity must go deeper. It must not only save but serve; it must bring God's compassion to the oppressed, as well as oppose the oppressors.

His mind clicked, and he dipped his pen in the inkwell. 'Almighty God has set before me two great objectives,' he wrote, his heart suddenly pumping with passion, 'the abolition of the slave trade and the reformation of manners.'

With those words, the offensive was launched for one of the epic struggles of modern history. God's man, called to stand against the entrenched evils of his day – the self-indulgent hedonism of a society pock-marked by decadence and the trade which underwrote those excesses: the barbaric practice of trafficking in human flesh for private gain.

From his discussions with Thomas Clarkson and others, Wilberforce knew the issue had to be faced head-on in Parliament. 'As soon as ever I had arrived thus far in my investigation of the slave trade,' he wrote, 'so enormous, so dreadful, so irremediable did its wickedness appear that my own mind was completely made up for the abolition. A trade founded in iniquity and carried on as this was, must be abolished, let the policy be what it might.'

Thus, throughout the wet autumn of 1787 he worked late into the night, joined by others who saw in the young politician the man God had raised up to champion their cause in Parliament.

There was Granville Sharpe, a hook-nosed lawyer with a keen mind. He was already well-known for his successful court case making slavery illegal in England herself – ironic in a time when her economic strength depended on slavery abroad.

Zachary Macaulay, a silent, patient researcher, sifted through extraordinary stacks of evidence, organizing facts to build damning indictments against the slave trade. A dedicated worker who regularly took pen in hand at four o'clock every morning, he became a walking encyclopaedia for the rest of the abolitionists. Whenever Wilberforce needed information, he would look for his quiet, heavy-browed friend, saying, 'Let us look it up in Macaulay!'

Thomas Clarkson, of course, was Wilberforce's right-hand man and scout, conducting various exhausting – and dangerous – trips to the African coast. He once needed some evidence from a particular sailor he knew by sight, though not by name. He searched through dozens of slave vessels in port after port, until finally, after searching 317 ships, he found his man.

Suddenly, in February of 1788, while working with these friends and others, Wilberforce fell gravely ill. Doctors warned he could not last more than two weeks. In Yorkshire the opposition party, cheered by such news, made plans to regain his seat in Parliament.

By March he was somewhat better, though not well enough to return to Parliament. He asked Pitt to introduce the issue of abolition in the House for him. Purely out of the warmth of their friendship, the prime minister agreed.

So in May of 1788, Pitt, lacking Wilberforce's passion but faithfully citing his facts, moved a resolution binding the House to discuss the slave trade in the next session.

His motion provoked a lukewarm debate, followed by a vote to duly consider the matter: those with interest in the trade were not worried about a mere motion to *discuss* abolition. Then Sir William Dolben, a friend of Wilberforce's, introduced a one-year experimental bill to regulate the number of slaves that could be transported per ship. After several MPs visited a slave ship lying in a London port, the debates grew heated, with cries for reform.

Now sensing the threat, the West Indian bloc rose in opposition. Tales of cruelty in the slave trade were mere fictions, they said; it was the happiest day of an African's life when he was shipped away from the barbarities of his homeland. The proposed measure, added Lord Penrhyn hysterically, would abolish the trade upon which 'two thirds of the commerce of this country depended'.

In response to such obstinate claims, Pitt himself grew passionate. Threatening to resign unless the bill was carried, he pushed Dolben's regulation through both Houses in June of 1788.

The success of Dolben's bill awakened the trade to the possibility of real danger. By the time a recovered Wilberforce returned to the scene, they were furious and ready to fight, shocked that Christian politicians had the audacity to press for religiously based reforms in the political realm. 'Humanity is a private feeling, not a public principle to act upon,' sniffed the Earl of Abingdon. Lord Melbourne angrily agreed, 'Things have come to a pretty pass when religion is allowed to invade private life.'

Wilberforce and the band of abolitionists knew that privatized faith, faith without action, meant nothing at all if they truly followed the God who mandated justice for the oppressed.

Wilberforce's first parliamentary speech for abolition on 12 May, 1789, shows the passion of his convictions, as well as his characteristic humility:

> When I consider the magnitude of the subject which I am to bring before the House – a subject, in which the interests, not of this country, nor of Europe alone, but of the whole world, and of posterity, are involved . . . it is impossible for me not to feel both terrified and concerned at my own inadequacy to such a task. But . . . I

march forward with a firmer step in the full assurance that my cause will bear me out . . . the total abolition of the slave trade . . .

I mean not to accuse anyone, but to take the shame upon myself, in common, indeed, with the whole Parliament of Great Britain, for having suffered this horrid trade to be carried on under their authority. We are all guilty – we ought all to plead guilty, and not to exculpate ourselves by throwing the blame on others.

But the passionate advocacy of Wilberforce, Pitt, and others was not sufficient to deter the interests of commerce in the 1789 session. The West Indian traders and businessmen pressured the House of Commons, which voted not to decide.

The House's vote to postpone action spurred Wilberforce to gather exhaustive research. He and his co-workers spent nine and ten hours a day reading and summarizing evidence. In early 1791 he again filled the House of Commons with his thundering yet sensitive eloquence.

Never, never will we desist till we have wiped away this scandal from the Christian name, released ourselves from the load of guilt under which we at present labour, and extinguish every trace of this bloody traffic, of which our posterity, looking back to the history of these enlightened times, will scarce believe that it has been suffered to exist so long a disgrace and dishonour to this country.

However, the slave traders were equally determined. One member argued:

> Abolition would instantly annihilate a trade, which annually employed upwards of 5,500 sailors, upwards of 160 ships and whose exports amount to 800,000 sterling; and would undoubtedly bring the West India trade to decay, whose exports and imports amount to upwards of 6,000,000 sterling, and which give employment in upwards of 160,000 tons of additional shipping, and sailors in proportion.

He paused, dramatically, and pointed up to the gallery, where a number of his slave-trading constituents watched approvingly, exclaiming brazenly, 'These are my masters!'

Another member, citing the positive aspects of the trade, drew a chilling comparison: the slave trade 'was not an amiable trade', he admitted, 'but neither was the trade of a butcher . . . and yet a mutton chop was, nevertheless, a very good thing.'

Incensed, Wilberforce and other abolitionists fought a bitter two-day battle; members shouted and harangued one another, as spectators and press watched the fray. By the time the votes were cast, in the terse summation of one observer, 'Commerce clinked its purse,' and Wilberforce and his friends were again defeated.

After their loss in 1791, Wilberforce and his growing circle of Christian colleagues, grieved and angered by the unconscionable complacency of Parliament, met to consider their strategy.

They were a varied group, marked by the common devotion to Christ and to one another. In addition to Wilberforce, the lawyer Sharpe, and researchers Clarkson and Macaulay, there was James Stephen, a handsome West Indian who had witnessed the evils of the slave trade firsthand. Stephen's passion for abolition could burst into fiery anger against those who propagated such evil.

Occasionally, in later years, he would even burst forth at Wilberforce when frustrated by the course of their battle.

Thomas Gisborne, a close friend of Wilberforce's at Cambridge, had lost touch with him after leaving the university. Now a clergyman and gifted orator, Gisborne wrote to Wilberforce, asking to join with him in the movement.

Henry Thornton, a Member of Parliament, was a calm, wealthy banker who brought managerial ability to the diverse group. He also became one of Wilberforce's closest friends, ready to weather any political storms or disappointments that might lie ahead.

These men, along with Thomas Babington, Charles Grant and writer Hannah More, were just a few of the personalities who gathered together to fight the slave trade. Committed to Christ as Lord above all, they began to form a bond based on more than the allegiance of a united political cause. They were, says one historian, 'a unique phenomenon – this brotherhood of Christian politicians. There has never been anything like it since in British public life.'

In 1792, as it became apparent that the fight for abolition would be long, Henry Thornton suggested to Wilberforce that they gather together at his home in Clapham, then a village four miles south of Westminster, convenient to Parliament yet set apart.

Thornton had thought out his plan and believed that living and worshipping together would draw the brotherhood closer to God and to one another. His home, 'Battersea Rise', was a lively Queen Anne house on the grassy Clapham Common. As friends came to live or visit, Thornton added extra wings. Eventually 'Battersea Rise' had thirty-four bedrooms, as well as a large, airy library designed by prime minister Pitt.

This oval, bookcase-lined room was the site of many

an intense prayer meeting and late-night discussion. Here, in the heart of the house, Thomas Clarkson related the horrors he had witnessed on his fact-finding missions to the African coast; here Henry Thornton led in prayer as all knelt on the polished floor. Here they met in hours-long 'cabinet councils', as they prepared for their parliamentary battles.

Wilberforce moved to Clapham to take up part-time residence in Thornton's home; then, after his marriage in 1797, he moved to Broomfield, a smaller house on the same property.

Clapham was also a place where the brothers sharpened and reproved one another. At several points the fiery James Stephen detailed several of Wilberforce's faults to him. To each such criticism Wilberforce replied, 'Go on, my dear sir, and welcome. . . . Openness is the only foundation and preservative of friendship.'

Such was Wilberforce's character – he welcomed not only the rebukes of his brothers, earnestly committing his failures to God, but he also brimmed over with the vitality which characterizes great saints.

In later years, this was often manifest in his attitudes towards his children and those of his colleagues. Sometimes he was 'as restless and volatile as a child himself', Henry Thornton's eldest daughter, Marianne, recalled. 'During the long and grave discussions that went on between him and my father and others he was most thankful to refresh himself by throwing a ball or a bunch of flowers at me, or . . . going off with me for a race on the lawn. . . . One of my first lessons was I must never disturb papa when he was talking or reading, but no such prohibition existed with Mr Wilberforce.'

Such was life at Clapham: a deeply committed and joyful community of Christian families, living in harmony as they pursued the great calls God had issued them; both the abolition of the slave trade and the reformation of a decadent society around them.

As the Clapham community analysed their battle in 1792, they were painfully aware that many of their colleagues in Parliament were puppets – unable or unwilling to stand against the powerful economic forces of their day.

So Wilberforce and his workers went to the people. In 1792 Wilberforce wrote, 'It is on the general impression and feeling of the nation we must rely . . . so let the flame be fanned.'

The abolitionists distributed thousands of pamphlets detailing the evils of slavery, spoke at public meetings and circulated petitions. The celebrated poet William Cowper had written *The Negro's Complaint*, a poem that was set to music and sung in many a fashionable drawing room. Josiah Wedgwood designed a cameo – which became the equivalent of a modern-day campaign badge – of a black man kneeling in bondage, whispering the plea that was to become famous, 'Am I not a man and a brother?'

They organized a boycott of slave-grown sugar, a tactic even Wilberforce thought could not work, but which gained a surprising following of some 300,000 across England.

Later in 1792, incredibly, Wilberforce was able to bring 519 petitions for the total abolition of the slave trade, signed by thousands of British subjects, to the House of Commons. As their movement rode on a surging tide of public popularity, Wilberforce's usual impassioned eloquence on the subject profoundly disturbed the House.

> In the year 1788 in a ship in this trade, 650 persons were on board, out of whom 155 died. In another , 405 were on board, out of whom were lost 200. In another there were on board

> 402, out of whom 73 died. When Captain Wilson was asked the causes of this mortality, he replied, that the slaves had a fixed melancholy and dejection; that they wished to die; that they refused all sustenance, till they were beaten in order to compel them to eat; and that when they had been so beaten, they looked in the faces of the whites, and said, piteously, 'Soon we shall be no more.'

Even the vested economic interests of the West Indian bloc could not gloss over these appalling facts or ignore the public support the abolitionists had gained. But again the slavers exercised their political muscle. The House moved that Wilberforce's motion should be qualified by the word 'gradually' and it was thus carried. The slave traders had no real fear of a bill which could be indefinitely postponed by that simple yet powerful word.

Though Wilberforce was wounded at yet another defeat, he had a glimmer of new hope. For the first time the House had voted for an abolition motion; with the force of the people behind the cause, it would only be a matter of time.

Suddenly, the events of the day reversed that hope. Across the English Channel the fall of the Bastille in 1789 had heralded the people's revolution in France. By 1792 all idealism vanished; the September massacres had loosed a tide of bloodshed in which the mob and the guillotine ruled France.

In England, fear of similar revolution abounded; any type of public agitation for reform was suspiciously labelled as 'Jacobinic', after the extreme revolutionaries who fuelled France's 'Reign of Terror'. This association, and ill-timed slave revolts in the West Indies, effectively turned back the tide of public activism for abolition.

The House of Commons, sensing this shift in the public mood, took the opportunity and rejected Wilberforce's motion for further consideration of the abolition of the trade. The House of Lords' attitude was summed up by the member who declared flatly, 'All Abolitionists are Jacobins.'

The abolitionists' success was quickly reversed; lampooned in popular cartoons and ridiculed by critics, Wilberforce could have no hope of success.

One can only imagine the grief and frustration he must have felt. Perhaps he went home late one night and sat at his old oak desk, staring into the flame of a single candle. 'Should I give up?' he might have thought. He sighed, flipping through his Bible. A thin letter fell from between the pages.

Wilberforce stared at the shaky handwriting. Its writer was dead; in fact, this letter was probably the last he had ever written. Wilberforce had read and reread it dozens of times, but never had he needed its message so deeply: 'My dear sir', it began,

> Unless the Divine power has raised you up to be as Athanasius contra mundum, I see not how you can go through your glorious enterprise, in opposing that execrable villainy, which is the scandal of religion, of England, and of human nature. Unless God has raised you up for this very thing, you will be worn out by the opposition of men and devils, but if God be for you who can be against you? Are all of them together stronger than God? Oh, be not weary of well-doing. Go on in the name of God, and in the power of his might, till even American slavery, the vilest that ever saw the sun, shall vanish away before it. That He that has guided you from your youth up may continue to

strengthen you in this and all things, is the prayer of,

Your affectionate servant,
John Wesley

'Be not weary of well-doing.' Wilberforce's mind clicked; he took a deep breath, carefully refolded the letter, and blew out the candle. He needed to get to bed – he had a long fight ahead of him.

Wilberforce doggedly introduced motions each year for abolition; each year Parliament threw them out. In late 1794 Wilberforce's advocacy for negotiating a peace in the war with France that had broken out the year before made him the subject of bitter public hostility. Even Pitt's friendship was temporarily shaken. The King disdained him, saying, 'I always told Mr Pitt they [the Clapham brothers] were hypocrites and not to be trusted.' Others used this opportunity to heap derision on his chief cause, abolition, and circulated rumours that Wilberforce, unmarried at the time, was a wife-beater and that his wife was a former slave.

Another abrupt reversal came early in 1796, after the fall of Robespierre in France, with the swing of public sentiment towards peace. Fickle popular favour again turned towards Wilberforce, reinforced in a surprising majority vote in the House of Commons for his annual motion for abolition. With surprising swiftness, victory was suddenly within his reach.

Unfortunately the third reading of the bill took place on the night a long-awaited comic opera opened in London. A dozen supporters of abolition, supposing that the bill would surely be voted in this time, skipped Parliament for the opera – and a grieving Wilberforce saw his bill defeated by just four votes.

So it went: 1797, 1798, 1799, 1800, 1801 – the years passed with Wilberforce's motions, thwarted and sabotaged by political pressures, compromise, personal illness and continuing war with France. By 1803, with the threat of imminent invasion by Napoleon's armies, the question of abolition was put aside for the more immediate concern of national security.

During those long years of struggle, however, Wilberforce and his friends never lost sight of their equally pressing objective – the reformation of English life.

John Wesley's indefatigable preaching over fifty years had produced a great revival a half-century earlier, with its effect still being felt in many areas, particularly among the poor. But many individuals within the Church of England were Christian in name only, religion simply part of their cultural dress.

Wilberforce would not accept a perversion of Christianity which treated Christ as Saviour but not as Lord. Of church people he wrote, 'If Christianity were disproved, their behaviour would alter little as a result.' Thus Sunday morning worship that did not manifest itself in daily holy living was hollow faith.

Given the prevailing attitudes of his day, Wilberforce knew he needed some dramatic ways to capture public attention and decided to ask King George III to reissue a 'Proclamation for the Encouragement of Piety and Virtue and for the Preventing of Vice, Profaneness and Immorality'. Though such proclamations were usually nothing but perfunctory political gestures, Wilberforce had discovered in his research that a similar statement issued by William and Mary had been used by local societies to successfully rally grass-roots support. Wilberforce believed the same thing could be repeated in his day.

Backed by Pitt and others, Wilberforce's proposal went to the King, who issued his proclamation on 1 June, 1787, citing his concern at the deluge of 'every kind of vice which, to the scandal of our holy religion, and to the evil example of our loving subjects, have broken upon this nation'.

Copies of the proclamation were distributed to magistrates in every county. Wilberforce mounted his horse and followed after them, calling on those in government and positions of leadership to set up societies to develop such a moral movement in Britain.

One prominent leader, Lord Fitzwilliam, laughed in Wilberforce's face – of course there was much debauchery and very little religion, he said, but after all, this was inevitable in a rich nation. 'The only way to reform morals,' he concluded, 'is to ruin purses.'

Even so, in many areas, the proclamation was received seriously. Magistrates held meetings to determine how to apply its guidelines, and long-ignored laws were dusted off and enforced.

Significantly, in his quest for reform, Wilberforce did not ignore the brutal and inequitable penal system of his day, which prescribed capital punishment for such 'heinous' offences as stealing hares or cutting down trees – applied towards men, women, and children alike. He urged reforms in the 'barbarous custom of hanging' though Wilberforce well knew that 'regulating the outward conduct did not change the hearts of men'. Reforming the general 'spirit of licentiousness' by turning men and women to Christ could provide the only cure for crime.

Wilberforce and his colleagues were sensitive to their critics' charge that the proclamation would be applied vigorously against the poor without affecting the rich. 'To expect to reform the poor while the opulent are corrupt,' wrote Hannah More, the Christian playwright, 'is to throw odours on the stream, while the springs are poisoned.' So Wilberforce and his companions focused much of their efforts on their own peers in the upper classes. It was to good effect, as increasing numbers began to crowd long-empty churches.

The aristocracy was also infiltrated by young servants and governesses who were converted in the campaign. One such governess took a special interest in young Anthony Cooper, who would later become the Earl of Shaftesbury, the crusading Christian politician who courageously pioneered the most sweeping social reforms of the nineteenth century.

The young Princess Victoria, later to lead her nation as one of history's best-known monarchs, was also affected, having an evangelical clergyman as her tutor. Later, Victoria's ladies-in-waiting would gather for prayer each morning before breakfast, lifting up the young queen in her leadership of what by mid-century would once again become a God-fearing nation.

In the campaign against the slave trade, Wilberforce had seen the enormous impact that small pamphlets had in shaping public opinion. So he set out to collect on paper his deepening convictions about holy living. Taking advantage of a six-week recess late in 1796, he finished work on a book he had been formulating for years. The title told the story: *A Practical View of the Prevailing Religious System of Professed Christians in the Higher and Middle Classes in this Country Contrasted with Real Christianity*.

He completed it in early 1797. His publisher, sceptical about the sales potential of such a narrow religious book in the market of the day, greeted him with less-than-encouraging words: 'You mean to put your name on the work?' Assured that Wilberforce did, the printer agreed on a cautious first run of 500 copies.

In a few days it was sold out. Reprinted again and again, by 1826 fifteen editions had been published in England and twenty-five in America, with foreign editions in French, Italian, Spanish, Dutch and German. It remains a classic today.

Wilberforce's friends were well-pleased. John Newton wrote, 'What a phenomenon has Mr Wilberforce sent abroad. *Such* a book by *such* a man and at *such* a time! A book which must and will be read by persons in the higher circles, who are quite inaccessible to us little folk, who will neither hear what we can say, nor read what we may write.'

In *A Practical View*, Wilberforce presented a clear biblical message of salvation and a call to holy living, as opposed to the insipid 'religion' so commonly practised. Wilberforce minced no words: to enter the Kingdom of God one must be born again. He wanted to impress his readers that 'all men must be regenerated by the grace of God before they are fit to be inhabitants of heaven, before they are possessed of that holiness without which no man shall see the Lord'. The true Christian is distinguished not by his church attendance but by his likeness to the holy, righteous Christ.

One prominent reader who sceptically picked up *A Practical View* and ended up being converted by it said simply, 'It led me to the Scriptures.' Countless thousands on two continents were similarly affected.

This book, written by a layman for lay people, revealed incredible theological insight and biblical understanding – evidence that Wilberforce had taken to heart the command to study, know and trust the infallible word of God.

His growing spiritual maturity served him well in handling political pressures of his day. During the winter of 1797, when he differed with Pitt regarding the war with France, he wrote in his journal, 'What conflicting passions yesterday in the House of Commons – mortification, anger, resentment – for such conduct in Pitt, though I ought to expect it from him and can well bear with his faults towards God – all these feelings working with anger at myself, from the consciousness that I was not what a Christian should be. . . . Yet even still I find my heart disposed to harbour angry thoughts. I have found the golden rule useful in quieting my mind and putting myself in Pitt's place.'

Wilberforce put into practice what he preached to others. Until his marriage in 1797, he regularly gave away a quarter of his income or more to the poor, Christian schools and those in special need. He paid the bills of those in prison under the harsh debt laws of the day, releasing them to live productive lives; he helped with the pension for life given to Charles Wesley's widow. In 1801, when the war with France and bad harvests created widespread hunger, Wilberforce gave away £3,000 *more* than his income.

Since the group at Clapham were mostly political conservatives, it may seem ironic to some that they were constantly engaged in schemes to aid the oppressed. They organized the Society for the Education of Africans, the Society for Bettering the Condition of the Poor, the Society for the Relief of Debtors (which over a five-year period obtained the release of 14,000 people from debtors' prisons), to mention a few.

Various Clapham members were involved in prison reforms, hospitals for the blind and help for war widows and distressed sailors. Zachary Macaulay, at one time worth £100,000, gave away all he had and died penniless.

That these two efforts – reforms of manners and abolition of the slave trade – remained linked through the years demonstrates the extraordinary spiritual insight of the Clapham sect. They understood the crucial interdependence of true spirituality and social reform. To attack social injustice while the heart of a nation remains corrupt is futile; to seek to reform the heart of a nation while injustice is tolerated ignores the lordship of Christ.

The years of battle had welded Wilberforce and the Clapham brothers into a tight working unit; with five of them serving as Members of Parliament, they exerted an increasingly strong moral pressure on the political arena of the day. Derisively labelled 'the saints', they bore the name gladly, considering their persecution a welcome reminder of their commitment not to political popularity, but to biblical justice and righteousness. James Boswell's bit of snide verse shows the bitter abuse heaped on Wilberforce by his enemies.

> Go, W— with narrow skull,
> Go home and preach away at Hull.
> No longer in the Senate cackle
> In strains that suit the tabernacle;
> I hate your little wittling sneer,
> Your pert and self-sufficient leer.
> Mischief to trade sits on your lip,
> Insects will gnaw the noblest ship.
> Go, W—, begone, for shame,
> Thou dwarf with big resounding name.

Wilberforce and his friends were undaunted as they prepared for the fight in Parliament in 1804. The climate had changed. The scare tactics of Jacobite association would no longer stick; and public sentiment for abolition was growing.

Thus the House of Commons voted for Wilberforce's bill by a decisive majority of 124 to 49 – but victory was short-lived. The slave traders were better represented in the House of Lords, which adjourned the bill until the next session.

In 1805, the House of Commons reversed its previous decision, voting against abolition, rejecting Wilberforce's bill by seven votes. A well-meaning clerk took him aside. 'Mr Wilberforce,' he said kindly, 'You ought not to expect to carry a measure of this kind – you and I have seen enough of life to know that people are not induced to act upon what affects their interests by any abstract arguments.' Wilberforce stared steely-eyed at the clerk. 'Mr Hatsell,' he replied, 'I *do* expect to carry it, and what is more, I feel assured I shall carry it speedily.'

Wilberforce went home in dismay, his heart torn by the notion of 'abstract arguments' when thousands of men and brothers were suffering on the coasts of Africa. 'I never felt so much on any parliamentary occasion,' he wrote in his diary. 'I could not sleep after first waking at night. The poor blacks rushed into my mind, and the guilt of our wicked land.'

Wilberforce went to Pitt to press for the cause. Pitt seemed sluggish. Wilberforce pushed harder, reminding him of old promises. Pitt finally agreed to sign a formal document for the cause, then delayed it for months. It was finally issued in September 1805. Four months later Pitt was dead.

Wilberforce felt his death keenly, longing that he might have seen the conversion of his dear friend. He said, 'I have a thousand times . . . wished and hoped that he and I might confer freely on the most important of all subjects, But now the scene is closed – for ever.'

William Grenville became prime minister. He and foreign secretary Fox were both strong abolitionists. With their power behind it, the passing of Wilberforce's bill appeared now only a matter of time.

After discussing the issue with Wilberforce, Grenville reversed the pattern of the previous twenty years and introduced the bill into the House of Lords first, rather than the House of Commons. After a bitter and emotional month-long fight, at 4 a.m. on the morning of 4 February, 1807, the bill was passed.

It then went to the House of Commons. On the night of its second reading, 22 February, a soft snow fell outside the crowded chambers. Candles threw flickering shadows on the cream-coloured walls; the long room was filled to capacity but unusually quiet. There was a sense that a moment in history had arrived. A force more powerful than kings and parliaments and slavers' profits had triumphed. Passions had been spent, and the moment was near that would mark the end of an epic twenty-year struggle.

Wilberforce, who had eaten supper earlier with Lord Howich, who was to introduce the bill, took his usual place quietly. He had written in his diary that morning with guarded confidence, 'God *can* turn the hearts of men,' but now, looking over the crowded room, he felt too aware of the defeats of the past to be certain of success.

Lord Howich, though an experienced speaker, opened the debate with a nervous, disjointed speech that reflected the tension in the chambers. Yet it did not matter; the opponents of abolition found they could do little to stem the decision about to be made.

One by one, members jumped to their feet to decry the evils of the slave trade and to praise the men who had worked so hard to end it. Speakers hailed Wilberforce and praised the abolitionists. Wilberforce, overcome, simply sat stunned. Waves of applause washed over him, and then as the debate came to its climax Sir Samuel Romilly gave a passionate tribute to Wilberforce and his decades of labour, concluding, 'when he should retire into the bosom of his happy and delighted family, when he should lay himself down on his bed, reflecting on the innumerable voices that would be raised in every quarter of the world to bless him; how much more pure and perfect felicity must he enjoy in the consciousness of having preserved so many millions of his fellow-creatures.'

Stirred by Romilly's words, the entire House rose, the members cheering and applauding Wilberforce.

Realizing that his long battle had come to an end, Wilberforce sat bent in his chair, his head in his hands, unable to even acknowledge the deafening cheers, tears streaming down his face.

The battle was won. As one by one the members cast their votes for abolition, the motion was carried by the overwhelming majority of 283 to 16.

Late that night, as Wilberforce and his friends burst out of the stuffy chambers and on to the snow-covered street, they frolicked about like schoolboys, clapping one another on the back, their joy spilling over. Much later, at Wilberforce's house, they crowded into the library, remembering the weary years of battle, rejoicing for their brothers on the African coast. Wilberforce, the most joyous of all, turned to the lined face of his old friend Henry Thornton. They had worked through years of illness, defeat, and ridicule for this moment. 'Well, Henry,' Wilberforce said with joy in his bright eyes, 'What do we abolish next?'

In the years that followed that night of triumph in 1807, a great spiritual movement swept across England like a fresh, cleansing breeze.

With the outlawing of the slave trade came an eighteen-year battle for the total emancipation of the slaves. Wilberforce continued as a leader of the cause in Parliament as well as working for reforms in the prisons, among the poor, and in the workplace. In poor health much of the time, he watched many of his friends die as the years rolled by. Others were raised up in their places. For though in the beginning of his crusade in 1787 he was one of only three Members of Parliament known as a committed Christian, by the end of his life more than 100 of his colleagues in the House of Commons and 100 members in the House of Lords shared that commitment.

Thus he could retire in 1825 knowing that God had

raised up others to continue the fight. His health grew steadily worse; finally in late July, 1833, Wilberforce lay helpless on his bed.

On the night of 26 July, the Bill for the Abolition of Slavery passed its second reading in the House of Commons, sounding the final death blow for slavery. Told the glad news, the old man raised himself on one bony elbow, then sank back, a quick smile crossing his lined face. 'Thank God,' he said, 'that I should have lived to witness a day in which England is willing to give twenty millions sterling for the abolition of slavery!'

By the following Sunday he was in a final coma; and early Monday morning, William Wilberforce went to be with the God he had served so faithfully.

In the summer of 1978, my wife Patty and I were in London, where I was delivering a lecture series at All Souls Church. When I noticed a free evening in my schedule, I asked my hosts to arrange a visit to Clapham, the place where Wilberforce and the 'saints' spent so much of their lives, praying, planning, and preparing for their glorious crusade.

Though I was a relatively new Christian, Wilberforce had already become a model for my life. Having experienced the lure of politics, power and position, I well understood the kind of inner struggles he must have endured. When he anguished over his decision to follow Christ, he wrestled with the most fearsome dragon: 'Pride is my great stumbling block,' he wrote in his diary.

I wrestled with the same dragon that unforgettable night in August of 1973 when a friend shared with me how Christ, the living God, had changed his life. All at once, my achievements, success and power seemed meaningless. For the first time in my forty years I realized that deep down in me was the most awful sin. I longed to be forgiven and cleansed. But the dragon of pride fought fiercely before it was slain in a flood of tears.

Wilberforce's life was also a magnificent inspiration for me in the ministry I had begun to prisoners. For his uncompromised commitment to Christ drove him all those years, one man taking his stand with a band of brothers for God's righteousness against the entire British Empire.

So I was anxious to visit the hallowed ground where Wilberforce and his friends had lived and worked.

A friend drove us through busy streets, heading south from the centre of London. Clapham, in Wilberforce's time a peaceful village a few miles from the city, was long ago swallowed up in the urban sprawl. We passed row after row of narrow, drab houses, and eventually came to the top of a small hill. 'There it is,' our friend exclaimed, pointing down a shabby street. 'That's where Henry Thornton's house used to be!'

'Used to be?' I replied in disbelief. 'Surely the Clapham sect's homes have been preserved as historic sites!'

'No,' my friend shook his head. 'Levelled long ago. People don't even know the exact location.'

I was stunned and disappointed. In the States, one finds markers at the site of obscure battlefields, monuments to long-forgotten pioneers, the footprints of screen stars preserved in cement.

We drove a short distance to the Clapham Green and stopped at an old soot-stained Anglican church. Our host had phoned ahead so the church rector was waiting to greet us.

'Wilberforce once preached in this pulpit,' he announced proudly as he led me up a rickety flight of wooden steps to an ornately carved oak pulpit. For an instant I felt a twinge of excitement to stand where this slight, little man with his thundering voice had stood.

Painted in the centre of a small stained glass window behind the altar was what the rector described as a 'quite good likeness' of Wilberforce. I squinted but could barely make it out. 'Is that all there is?' I asked, my disappointment deepening. 'Oh, no!' the rector replied, leading me to a side wall where a small brass plaque was mounted in honour of the Clapham 'saints'. A pile of booklets about Wilberforce and his companions was stacked on a nearby table under a sign '50p each'. That was it.

I'll never forget the scene, nor my emotions, as we left that little parish church. The cool, misty air sent chills through me. 'After all those men accomplished,' I mumbled, 'surely more could have been done to honour their memory.'

As we walked past the rows of dreary houses lining Clapham Green, my host cautioned, 'Not a good area to walk at night.' It didn't matter; I felt I had already been robbed, somehow cheated.

Suddenly I stopped and stared across the green. In my mind's eye I began to see row upon row of black men and women walking right across the soft grass. I could hear the clanging of their chains as they fell from their arms and legs.

Of course, of course, I thought. Clapham is just what Wilberforce and his brothers would want. No spires of granite or marble rising into the sky. No cold statues or lifeless buildings in their honour. Rather the monument to Wilberforce and his friends is to be found in the freedom enjoyed by hundreds of millions of black people, liberated from bondage by a band of men who gave their all in following Christ.

Look at Africa today. It was Wilberforce and his friends who financed the first missionaries. Now Christianity, once the religion of the people's oppressors, is exploding across the continent, growing faster than anywhere else in the world.

The legacy of Wilberforce goes beyond even abolition and Africa. Taking a longer view of history, we can now see that he was a man standing in the gap at a crucial point in the history of Christendom – and the world. For in the late eighteenth century the Age of Reason dawned on the Continent. Humanist 'enlightenment' was fast seizing the minds of the intelligentsia.

That is what sparked off the bloody French Revolution. The revolution to end the unholy rule of divinely ordained tyrant kings would finally usher in man's utopia to reign on earth.

The main line of defence against the surging tides of Enlightenment humanism had to be drawn in Britain. Where else? In the colonies, where a new nation was just taking root, fewer than five per cent attended church. Rough frontiersmen had little time for religious niceties – and Enlightenment writers like Thomas Paine were profoundly influencing America's founding fathers.

But Britain was, spiritually speaking, sinking sand. The church was apostate, the whole nation wallowing in self-indulgent decadence. But it was there that Wilberforce and his companions took their stand clinging to biblical truth, resisting barbaric injustice and striving to change the heart of a nation.

The eminent historian Will Durant once wrote that the great turning point of history was when 'Christ met Caesar in the arena – and Christ won'. Well might he have added that fifteen centuries later, Christ met vice and vested interests in Britain – and Christ won.

For out of Wilberforce's effort came a great spiritual movement in England. Social reforms swept beyond abolition to clean up child employment laws, poorhouses, prisons, to institute education and health care for the poor. Church attendance swelled. Evangelicalism flourished, and later in the century missionary movements sent Christians fanning across the globe.

Christianity took such firm root in America as to convert a near-lawless frontier into a city upon a hill. The rising tides of Enlightenment humanism were stemmed.

Monument to Wilberforce? Yes, the monument is a living legacy, found not only in the lives of millions of free men and women, but in the spiritual heritage of Christians everywhere.

Wilberforce has left a special legacy for today's Christians, caught up as so many are in the illusion that military might and political institutions are all-powerful. In the conclusion to his masterful book, *A Practical View*, Wilberforce wrote,

> I must confess equally boldly that my own solid hopes for the well-being of my country depend, not so much on her navies and armies, nor on the wisdom of her rulers, nor on the spirit of her people, as on the persuasion that she still contains many who love and obey the Gospel of Christ. I believe that their prayers may yet prevail.